A Grandmother's

Book

A Grandmother's ABC Book

Kathy Ewing

photographs by Margaret Ewing

SHANTI ARTS PUBLISHING

BRUNSWICK, MAINE

A Grandmother's ABC Book

Published by Shanti Arts Publishing

Designed by Shanti Arts Designs

Shanti Arts LLC
193 Hillside Road
Brunswick, Maine 04011
shantiarts.com

Printed in the United States of America

ISBN: 978-1-956056-86-0 (softcover)

Library of Congress Control Number: 2023935880

To Hank and Celia

In memory of Connie Carter Wade (1963–2022)

Acknowledgments

THANKS TO SEWBABY, INC., FOR THE ALPHABET TAKE-Along Book pattern. Despite my whining and teeth-gnashing, the book is actually "easy to sew," as advertised, for anyone even slightly more skilled than I.

Special thanks to Margaret Ewing and Tim Freeman for finding each other, marrying, and having beautiful (as we now know) babies. From the first, you've been excellent offspring, and now you're exceedingly excellent parents.

Thanks to Christine Cote and Shanti Arts for taking on this hodgepodge of a book. And thanks to my writing group for encouraging me in what they affectionately (I think) term "my project."

Special thanks to Jewel Moulthrop, dear to me both as an editor and precious friend.

And thanks to John Ewing, another astute editor, for his advice, love, and support. Without him, there would be no Margaret, no twins, and no book.

Beginnings

IN MID-SEPTEMBER 2020, I CALLED YOUR MOTHER TO FIND out more about the camping trip that she and your dad had taken with friends over Labor Day weekend. She called back and described three exhausting hours of canoeing in choppy waters to reach an island in Lake George, where they hiked, ate, and slept in tents.

Elisa and Evan, friends you might know your entire life, were sleeping in a different tent. They had all been warned about a friendly raccoon family that lived near the campsite. They never saw the critters, but Elisa and Evan heard the raccoons breathing right by their heads just outside their tent. Evan couldn't sleep because of raccoon breath.

As this story ended, your mom suggested we switch to a Zoom call, so that your dad could see how my new computer microphone was working. This was in itself a sign of the times, because six months earlier, before the start of the pandemic, we would have been flummoxed at the very suggestion of Zoom. Now we were old hands.

Still, it seemed an odd suggestion; why not merely say that the new mic was working fine? But maybe not so odd because your dad is interested in technology. When we connected, they in New York and we in Cleveland, I jawed on inanely about the new mic, which was also a camera. I had purchased it for a Zoom talk I had delivered that week about my recently published book. "The picture isn't that great," your dad commented, also a little inanely. How much more could we find to say about the new microphone and camera? Why were we talking about them at all?

Thankfully, your mom interrupted. "Where's Dad? Call him to the computer to say hi," she said. Again, a little odd. Your grandfather would have nothing interesting to add to the microphone discussion.

After he sat down next to me in front of the computer and said hi, your mom announced that they had news. "Ah," I dimly realized that this call was about something.

"We-e-e-ll," your mom said. "I'm pregnant."

We responded with something like, "Oh, my gosh! Great news!"

Then she said, "Wait. There's more. I had an ultrasound today, and they showed me two. Two babies." She held up two fingers to make sure we understood.

I put my hands to my face and said, "What? Twins?" Your parents had discovered only hours before that there were two of you.

We learned other facts as they were known at that time. No info as to gender. Due date March 27, but twins usually arrive early. You mom had been feeling queasy, but as she was entering your second trimester, she was beginning to feel better. She was working furiously at the same time to help reopen her school in the midst of the COVID pandemic. "It's like we're creating a brand-new school," she said.

Because of the lockdown, then in its fifth month, this "new" school would entail at-home learning via computer for the first weeks. It involved complicated scheduling and arranging an online orientation for freshmen. This was what your mom was doing while you were gestating. Also dog-sitting off and on for Bella, the beloved dog belonging to your Brooklyn friends Jamie and Alicia. And strenuous canoeing.

She planned to work as long into March as possible and then take maternity leave for the summer. Your dad, working at home because of the pandemic, would begin his enviable three-month paternity leave in the fall when she went back to work.

We expressed more joy. Before signing off, I said something like, "Haven't I been good? I've never asked you about grandchildren, have I?" Your mom agreed that I had been very good.

Aside from the pandemic, your parents' timing was fortuitous. The Latin classes I normally teach at Cleveland State had been canceled due to low enrollment. Your grandfather recently retired as film curator for the Cleveland Museum of Art. He continued to work nonstop at his other job, programming movies for the Cleveland Institute of Art Cinematheque, but he was quarantined at home with a flexible schedule. That meant we could travel to New York City when you were born, or at least when you were very, very little. A lot would depend on when COVID vaccines became available. Flying was inadvisable without that protection.

Your grandfather was very happy, like me, although the news made him feel old. Your own dad was excited about having twins. Your mom admitted to feeling shocked. I texted them after our conversation to say that they were going to be great parents. Your dad texted me back that they were going to sell the baby born second so they would have extra money to raise the first one right. Your mom texted, "Don't listen to him."

I called my friend Katie before going to bed because she knew exactly how much I have wanted this to happen.

I had been waiting for you, or for babies like you. I had told my friends constantly that I never imagined I would be one of those people who waited impatiently for their kids to have kids, but there I was. Your parents had been married for almost five years and were soon to turn thirty-five. Most of their married friends had kids already. Because your parents hadn't mentioned kids for a long time, I worried that maybe they had decided against having a family. I wouldn't ask because if they didn't want kids, I didn't really want to know. More importantly to me, your grandpa and I were about to turn seventy, and at my back I could always hear, not raccoons, but time's winged chariot hurrying near. I wanted to be a strong, healthy grandmother. Your grandfather's mom and dad were stellar grandparents, and I aspired to be like them. I was always doing the math in my head; with luck, I'd be in my mid-eighties when you would be in high school.

Of course the news made me happy, but also a little worried because a twin pregnancy is unusual and caring for two babies challenging. Not to mention bearing not one but two babies during a coronavirus pandemic. This was my daughter we're talking about. I also felt sad that your parents already had a plan in place for remaining in NYC next fall. I wanted all of you nearer to me in Cleveland. This was another yearning, like the one for grandchildren, that I tried not to dump onto your mom and dad.

A couple of days later, I had gotten out of bed and started getting dressed before I thought of you. Then I remembered the Zoom call and suddenly felt happy. Your mom shared the news with aunts Barbara, Penni, Marge, and Betsey, and cousins Katy and Julie. The aunts all texted me congratulations, and Aunt Barbara called and talked to your grandfather for a long time. She wished him a happy Grandparents Day, because that's what it was.

I sent your other grandma congratulations. She was overwhelmed because Aunt Meagan, your dad's sister, was also pregnant. Her baby, due in November, will always be three or four months older than you, depending on when you are all actually born. Grandma Connie would go from no grandchildren to three grandchildren in only four months. She was itching to talk to your dad's sisters, Meagan and Ashley, but your dad hadn't told them yet, and she was supposed to keep the secret for a little while longer.

Excited as I was, I found that you did not seem real to me. You remained amorphous and blobby, like your ultrasound pictures. Part of this unreality stemmed from the distance between us. I wanted to be in closer touch to find out exactly how your mom was feeling day to day. If I lived nearer and there were no pandemic, I could have gone to doctor appointments with her sometimes. Was her pregnancy showing yet? Did she feel you moving?

After a few weeks, we received news that zapped you into sharper focus: you were a girl and a boy. In our time, we're learning to be sensitive to people across a spectrum of genders—nonbinary, transgender, and so on. Even so, in the fall of 2020, we were very interested in who you were and everything about you. Everyone was happy to have a boy baby and a girl baby. My texts to family and friends said, "1 girl baby + 1 boy baby = 2 babies."

It was not your genders that were making people happy, though. My friends were happy for me because they knew I had been ready for a grandchild for a while. Beyond that, most of us were going through a pretty hard time. All around us swirled dark jokes about how we couldn't wait for 2020 to end. You'll learn a lot about the coronavirus pandemic as you grow and hear the stories grown-ups will tell, and when you go to school and study history, you will learn about the feelings of anxiety and sadness that settled over everyone. People were dying of COVID, the illness caused by the new virus, and we were all trying to avoid becoming sick and spreading the virus unknowingly. We read stories of couples dying within hours of each other, in separate hospital rooms, with no family members allowed to visit. We were inundated with news of overtaxed hospitals and first responders in danger. Politics made people disagree about how to address the crisis or even about whether there was a crisis. Some people believed the virus was a hoax, that the illness wasn't very serious, and the measures to counteract it were too drastic. In an election year, these disagreements made for a lot of shouting in presidential debates and on the streets and in Congress. Very stressful for everyone.

•

To distract myself during these hard times, I began a project: sewing a fabric alphabet book for you. As I cut and sewed and cursed at my machine, I didn't have to think about the insidious virus. My thoughts meandered instead: imagining you two, reminiscing about your mom and Uncle Doug, reacting to the news or the classic rock on the radio, and obsessing over the looming election and Donald Trump. These wandering thoughts inspired a spin-off project: to describe the creation of the alphabet book, letter by letter, as it came together. By the time you read these alphabet-inspired musings—a sort of grown-up book addressed to precious babies—the fabric book may have fallen apart. It may be lost. I've never had abundant confidence in my sewing skills, so who knows how it will hold up. Maybe you'll have no memory of it.

The letter A marks the beginning of both the fabric alphabet book and the one you're holding in your hands. They were created in tandem, writing interposed with sewing, filling up the long days of lockdown when it seemed dangerous to go to the grocery store or grab a latte. This book skips around a lot during one year, from the lockdown in March 2020 to March 2021, the month of your birth.

It's addressed to you in utero, merely inches long, but growing fast. You may be reading it years into the future, knowing it was written for you. Maybe you'll wonder what it was like to live through this strange year and what your grandparents were doing and thinking while we waited for you.

We've "all gone and had ourselves an experience," a friend once wrote to my father, your great-grandfather. We're still going through something, even as I write. That something involves a highly contagious disease, and though it sounds morbid, I can't help occasionally imagining I might die of COVID before this book is finished. I don't dwell on it, but some dread always lurks around us. I guess if you're reading this now, I didn't die, or at least I completed both books in time.

You should know, though, that you were prenatally cheering people up, even people outside of the family. When I shared news of you, everyone felt better. Babies inspire hope, which everybody needed then. A friend I often ran into at my favorite coffee shop, where we were allowed to sit only outside, was so delighted that her face crinkled up in a big grin. "So good to hear some good news!" she said over and over again. She meant you. You were the good news.

A Is for Apple

THE LETTER A SIGNIFIES BEGINNINGS, NOT ONLY IN THE alphabet but in phrases like "from A to Z." When God says "I am the Alpha and the Omega" in the book of Revelation, he/she denotes the beginning and the ending and everything in between; *alpha* being the first letter of the Greek alphabet and *omega* being the last.

For us modern English speakers, A always stands for *apple*.

As you might expect, it's the first letter I cut out for your alphabet book. I select a green print fabric for the A. For the apple, I use a remnant of red fabric I used to make a living room pillow a couple of years ago. It's dark red with black flecks and so looks like a deep red delicious apple, the kind your Uncle Doug likes.

Doug, a few years older than your mom, lives with us in our Cleveland Heights home, which it amuses him to call it our "starter home," even though we've owned it for almost forty years. Doug, at the time of this writing, works at a nearby retirement facility, which has had cases of COVID and even a few deaths. Fortunately, he hasn't been exposed himself or brought the virus home to us, his aging parents.

When we heard of your existence, and a few weeks after we learned that you are one boy and one girl, someone pointed out to me that in the dusky future in which you two will grow up, gender categories may be obsolete. Forgive my retro boomer self here, clinging to old definitions of female and male and other matters. I'll like you whatever your sexual identity.

•

Anyway, apples. We have a family tradition of taking a fall drive to fetch pumpkins and apples and cider, dear to your grandfather's heart. He loves everything autumnal, including Halloween, but especially cider, whose natural partner, to him, is doughnuts. We have many photos of your mom and Uncle Doug, along with Grandma and Poppie Ewing (your great-grandparents) amidst pumpkins and straw bales at orchards and roadside stands in the countryside east of where we live.

Because of the pandemic, we have taken several of these drives this year. Cooped up most of the time, we relish venturing out in our safely enclosed cars. Often the weather is stunningly beautiful—sunny azure skies, brilliant white clouds, and unseasonably warm temperatures, which blessed us for weeks. Your grandfather and I have walked in far-flung parks, along with Roxie, our tiny white Maltese mix. Doug comes along if he's not working.

One recent day, we journeyed about half an hour to rural Geauga County and walked around Bass Lake. The weather had finally taken a turn, and the wind was chilly enough for skinny Roxie to need her sweater. After a cold walk, we drove a little farther east to Sage's Apple Farm in Chardon. We had to stop to ask a pizza delivery guy for directions, because my phone didn't have enough charge left to help us find the way. We purchased yet one more gallon of cider to add to our supply at home. I bought tomatoes—delicious home-grown ones that I served later that day for dinner—and maple-coated popcorn, which I nearly finished off that evening.

Our bags of apples at home were still almost full from the previous week's drives to Patterson's and Eddy's, two other orchards east of us. But that didn't stop Doug from purchasing a peck of those deep red delicious ones, and I brought home a bag of Cortlands. I cooked up some good applesauce from these, which I shared with my friend Katie, whose mom had been sick so I've tried to assist with occasional food drop-offs.

Grandpa picked out a pumpkin on that trip, which he planned to carve on Halloween. Of course, I have no idea at this point what you will call your grandfather. "Grandpa" sounds disconcerting to me because he's Dad or John to us. Grandpa is what we called our own grandfathers, or even one of your mom or dad's granddads, but I guess every grandparent goes through this adjustment. I'll call him Grandpa in this book, jarring though the word is to me.

Grandpa loves cider so much. When your mom and uncle were young, we used to bring several gallons of different types of cider home. Grandpa would pour each one in a separate glass to set up a big taste test and place them before Doug and your mom and me. Which one did we like best? Which did we think was Patterson's, which was Eddy's, which was Sage's? Which was the no-name supermarket brand? There was no prize. No actual upshot. It was just a thing we did. We still make jokey references to the Cider Taste Test.

On this trip we never stopped for donuts, and for Grandpa cider requires donuts. Hence, once we got home I took the drastic step of making donuts. It's a messy job. You pour an abundance of vegetable oil into a pot, and when the donuts are done you're left with a massive amount of used oil—with bits of burned donut floating around in it—to dispose of. In the past, I've tried reusing the oil, but the less said about that the better. Heating the oil to the right temperature is also problematic; it can't be too hot but it must definitely be hot enough! It has to be just right, exactly like Goldilocks. Fortunately, with my fancy digital thermometer, I started out at the right temperature but never rechecked it. The oil near the end of the cooking wasn't hot enough, and the donuts absorbed a lot of oil. Even so, they tasted pretty good, and Grandpa and Doug liked them. I did too. I put a little cinnamon and nutmeg in the batter so they ended up with that distinctive cakey donut taste. I shook them in a bag with sugar and cinnamon before we dove in.

•

The apple in your book, on the A page, occasions my first error. I fuse interfacing to the back of the apple, but it is regular interfacing, sticky only on the side facing the apple fabric, not on the side where it needs to be fused to the page of the book. I couldn't find the double stick interfacing at the craftstore but eventually order it online and apply it to the apple. Now the apple sticks to the page, and I stitch around it in red.

I like the general effect of the finished page. The apple's stem comes from some Christmas fabric with cardinals on a gray background with a pattern of twigs. The green leaf is cut from a big swatch of fabric from which I made some napkins and placemats a few years ago. The whole thing is simple and easily put together. Not too many parts. My error, like so many errors, is fixable.

A is the start of everything. The beginning of the alphabet as well as the beginning of *alphabet*. The beginning of this book.

B Is for Bear

AT FIRST, PRODUCING THIS PAGE IS UNEVENTFUL. I CHOOSE the gingerbread cookie fabric purchased in order to make Christmas masks. That sewing project gave me the confidence to take on this book project.

Masks are ubiquitous right now. Or perhaps I should say we wish they were ubiquitous. Everyone's supposed to wear a mask when they're out in public. This is to protect themselves from other people's possible coronavirus and to protect others from the infection we might unknowingly be carrying. I sewed masks obsessively last March when mask mandates first came down from our state government. I shared them with family, with Doug's coworkers at the retirement community, and with the young women who work at my favorite cafe, the Stone Oven. Then I had the idea of making everyone in the family a Christmas mask to wear after Thanksgiving. I chose various red and green fabrics, white snowflakes, and the cardinal fabric I mentioned on the A page. Each mask was reversible, so I could mix and match them many different ways. I mailed them during Thanksgiving weekend, so they'd arrive as soon as the Christmas season began.

The gingerbread cookie fabric was intended for the kids' masks. By kids, I mean your second cousins, Gillian, Phillip, and Stephen. (The oldest cousin, David, qualified for an adult mask. He started high school this year.) I bought some snowman fabric, too, so the kids' masks mostly had snowmen on one side and gingerbread girls and boys on the other. I think I was under some kind of delusion when I chose the gingerbread fabric for the B page though. It's brownish like a bear, but it's covered in gingerbread boys and girls, not bears. I vaguely imagined they were teddy bears without actually thinking about it. People these days are talking a lot about "COVID brain," a general fuzziness and vague forgetfulness, which might explain this choice. I thought cookies were bears in some weird way. Anyway, the fabric has a kid vibe going for it. I like the red B on the page.

At first all goes smoothly. The B page goes with Y page, side by side. That is, B is the alphabet's second letter, and the Y is the second to the last. The book starts with A and Z side by side. Then I work my way forward through the beginning of the alphabet and backward from the end.

My mistake is to put the B on the left and the Y on the right. You can understand why I would do that, right? B comes before Y. But this arrangement is wrong. After fusing them to the book fabric and stitching around them, I try setting the page next to the A and Z page, but to my dismay the book reads "A Z C", and at the end B comes before Z. So upsetting! I've done what I worried about doing from the beginning: assembling the book incorrectly. I check the corners of the page where I wrote in pencil the appropriate letters. Sure enough, those corners say Y and B, not B and Y. I didn't check before pressing and sewing.

Later, I lie in bed imagining how to fix this. I can cut the page in half, though the thought of such drastic and irrevocable action frightens me. Then I have to switch the pages, putting Y on the left. I also have to cut out some extra canvas fabric to fill in the gap, because stitching the pages together will require an inch of seam allowance. I keep picturing it over and over and settle on cutting out two inches of fabric to rejoin the pages in the correct order. I finally fall asleep.

The next day comes, and I can't tackle this task first thing in the morning because I need some time to summon my courage. After a few hours, I steel myself to do what I have to do. I cut. I switch the letters, Y on the left and B on the right. I sew them together with the extra fabric in the middle and press them. The finished width of the pages, eighteen inches, is right. The only problem is those extra seams near the center of the pages. I show the pages to Grandpa, who says they look fine. Enjoined to look at every page as I finish them, he perfects a benign, distracted "very nice."

Here's that lesson again: mistakes can usually be remedied.

•

Many people know that our B comes from the second letter of the Greek alphabet, *beta*. If you put the first two letters of the Greek alphabet, *alpha* (A) and *beta* (B), together, you make *alphabet*.

I learned about types of writing decades ago in a linguistics class at Kent State University, and I even remember some of it. The earliest kind of writing is called pictographic—"writing in pictures." For example, if you buy five oxen from a neighbor, you might finalize the deal by drawing five bulls on paper, or more accurately, on animal skin. These are pictographs. After a few generations of drawing bulls on animal skin, people gradually simplified and stylized the shape because drawing fully detailed bulls became tiresome. Eventually, they might have ended up with a sort of triangle shape for the head with horns sticking out. Turn our capital A sideways, and that's what you see. It is roughly the shape of the A beginning the Phoenician word *aleph*, which means "ox." Similarly, the Greek letter *beta* derives from the Phoenician *beth*, meaning "house." It's harder to see a house in our B, but ancient versions look something like the floor plan of a house. You see the actual word today in Hebrew in Beth Israel Hospital, which means the House of Israel hospital. *Alpha* and *beta* are used in English to signify first and second and sometimes strong and weak, as in alpha male or B movie.

I remember being fascinated by how these hieroglyphs, these pictograms evolved into phonetic letters, how eventually the *aleph* and the *beth* came to signify the A sound and the B sound. This was a giant step in human history because instead of countless pictograms representing the billions of objects in the world, a phonetic alphabet can represent the word for every single thing and idea. Alexander and Nicholas Humez in their book, *Alpha to Omega: The Life and Times of the Greek Alphabet* (1983), describe the alphabet as "arguably the most influential and far-reaching of humankind's many ingenious inventions to date." Employed also in mathematical and musical notation, the alphabet is "an invention staggering in its implications."

These ancient alphabets evolved into our familiar letters approximating the sounds of our speech. That's what I'm looking at on my screen as I write in October of 2020: the alpha-beta—the twenty-six letters that combine and recombine to make all the words, more than 170,000, in English. And all the words in written French, Spanish, Italian, Dutch, and many other languages. This brilliant human invention is what you'll be contemplating, at some point in the future, in this book about a little cloth book created to introduce you to the letters of the alphabet.

C Is for Cat

A CAMEL MIGHT BE MORE LINGUISTICALLY APPROPRIATE than a cat. According to the philosopher Bertrand Russell, the letter's Greek ancestor, *gamma* (Γ), comes from the Phoenician *gimel*, or "camel." Other sources connect *gamma* to a similar word meaning "walking stick." You can see that in the shape, right? Cutting out and stitching a walking stick would be simpler than a camel, so I'd probably opt for that etymology if I had the opportunity to choose. The letter C shares its history with the letter G, as you'll see when we get there. In the meantime, note that poor little C is actually superfluous, in that K and S pretty much cover its sounds. For that reason, Benjamin Franklin's phonetic alphabet, one of his many inventions, eliminated the C altogether.

Our pattern chooses the traditional cat for C. Creating the cat itself proceeds much more smoothly than the dog, as you'll soon see. For both of them, however, the eyes are a struggle. It's hard for me to cut out perfect ovals for the whites of the eyes. Then it is challenging to situate the dark pupils on the whites so that the animal doesn't appear deranged. Finally, it's tricky to place the eyes symmetrically and pleasingly on the animal's face. Lots of hazards for my unsteady hands! I experiment with using a gold-brown flowery fabric for the eyes, but the cat looks demonic. I could have made the cat itself black (it's now approaching Halloween), but I didn't think of that until just now.

The cat also requires what the instructions term a "smile." And whiskers as well. I intend to try embroidering them, because I can rip out embroidery if it goes cattywampus (so to speak), but fabric marker would make my convulsive wobbles permanent. I end up mixing the two media. First, I try machine stitching instead of hand embroidering. The line straight down and the "smile" to the right look fine, but I can't make the smile on the left match. I pull out several lines of stitches and end up using the fabric pen. The cat's smile is a little wavery.

•

You're being born into a family that generally loves dogs more than cats, though some of us like cats and dogs about equally. I, for example, would adopt a cat if your grandfather, your mom and dad, and your Uncle Doug were not allergic to them. You may be inheriting the same allergy! My long-lived old cat Gray Girl was still residing at my childhood home on 55th Street in Canton when Grandpa and I began dating. When he'd hang out at our house, she'd climb up next to him and sidle onto his lap. Cats have a way of cozying up to people who don't like them.

Similarly, Gray Girl enjoyed nestling beside my mom, your great-grandmother, in her TV-watching chair. My mom would make disgruntled noises but not push her off. She routinely called the cat a pest and otherwise pretty much ignored her. When I once alluded to her not liking cats, she replied indignantly, "Who says I don't like cats? I always had a cat!" News to me. Your great-grandma was a frustrating person. I wrote a whole other book about that.

Anyway, I haven't owned a cat since because I was already dating your grandpa when Gray Girl died. Back then we were living pretty far apart. I was at graduate school in Kent, and he lived in Canton and worked at the Stark County District Library. In the 1970s, long distance phone calls were expensive, so we would often send each other notes instead of calling. I once composed a mock love note to him from Gray Girl and tucked clumps of Gray Girl's fur in the envelope. The fur ended up all over his clothes, causing some sneezes and watery eyes. He was not amused.

Despite the allergy, Gray Girl eventually won him over. "She was a nice cat," he admits grudgingly. Years ago, I thought that if I outlived your granddad, I could have a cat in my old age, but then I realized that because both your parents and Doug are also allergic, and maybe you as well, no one would ever be able to visit me. You can receive a shot of an antibody improbably named tezepelumab to control your allergic symptoms. I will not attempt an etymology for that word. I'm pretty sure that no family member is inclined to indulge me by getting inoculated. Scientists have also been testing a cat vaccine called HypoCat, which means "less cat." The Purina company has introduced a new cat chow that reduces allergenic dander in cats, but who knows how well it works? Alas, all probably too late for me, but maybe when you're grown up, all allergies will have been cured.

Your great-aunt Marge, my older sister, has lots of cats at her farm in Minerva. Some are strictly barn cats, but some are privileged indoor cats. She has so many that she was afraid to mail the blankets she crocheted for you, fearing they're chock-full of cat dander. At first, I assume that she's concerned for your parents' allergies, but then I realize she's thinking of you. Web MD, in fact, explains that though an allergic tendency can be hereditary, exposure to allergens before the age of two might avert an eventual allergy. In any event, it seemed to me that a good laundering would do the trick, but those reassurances took time to settle in. Marge eventually washed the blankets and sent them to me for another washing. I will deliver them safe and allergen free, I hope, to you in New York.

Marge has traditionally named all her dogs and cats after members of the Rock and Roll Hall of Fame. The dog she named Gladys, for example, was found as a puppy in a box by the side of the road with her three brothers, the Pips. One of those puppies became our beloved family dog Shucks, whom we acquired when your mom was only nine years old. After Shucks died in 2011, your grandfather bought a headstone for the dog's backyard grave for Christmas. We all cried when I opened it. Your own dad, generally unsentimental about animals, has expressed bemusement at this extravagant gesture, but then he never knew Shucks.

As I write, Marge's cat Brenda Lee (2002 Rock Hall inductee) is ailing. Marge thought that the cat would have to be put to sleep a couple of weeks ago, but Brenda has rallied somewhat. She spends her life indoors on Marge's or Marge's boyfriend Ed's lap. Or she lies under the bed in the darkness by herself, perhaps because she heard tell there was a pandemic going around.

Your dad's side of the family boasts some true cat lovers. Aunt Ashley works with a rescue group and frequently posts irresistible pictures on Facebook to tempt her friends to adopt. Aunt Meagan also loves cats and has at least one now. Your mom and dad don't particularly love cats.

•

Aside from my problems centering the cat's eyes, the C page goes fine, for a while. I am very pleased to find the pawprint fabric for this page and the next. Joann's and Walmart sell pieces of fabric about eighteen inches square, which I use throughout the book when my own remnants aren't ideal. But then, inevitably, they arrive—the sewing machine problems. Most people who've sewn, especially marginally skilled ones like me, have been harassed by sewing machines into cursing, crying, and giving up on their simple shower curtain or eighth-grade home economics blouse because of snarled thread and broken needles.

When I was growing up, we had an old Kenmore sewing machine, the brand name for Sears department stores, a destination you'll have missed entirely because, as of this writing, only about thirty-five stores (out of some 3,000 in its heyday) remain open. All of the relatives—your great-grandparents and all the rest—grew up knowing Sears—founded in 1892—its ubiquitous catalogue, and its tools, clothes, and appliances. As malls have declined and online shopping has flourished, Sears and its stodgy image have gradually faded into memory.

Our Kenmore machine was not old-old, as in a beautiful black antique with a foot pedal, but circa 1950s. I found one with the same weird salmon color on eBay with an asking price of $350. The California seller described the model as "mid-century," which is about right. Ours came with a tweedy black and white carrying case. I kept this sewing machine as an adult for many years, in a corner of the basement that I claimed for my sewing. That's where I created Halloween costumes for your mom and Doug, and a pink toddler outfit for your mom that she would never wear, a persnickety fashionista from the start. Your mom also used that machine to produce a giant pillow for Shucks to lie on, currently enjoyed by his successor, Roxie.

That machine was quite temperamental, or else I was too impatient. Finally, a leaky pipe in the basement dripped all over it from above, and I gave up. I left the machine out by the curb a day before our trash pick-up day, and a gleaner harvested it, as people often do in our neighborhood. I suspected then that I would never be sewing again. When I took home economics, as all girls did in the 1960s, I had to finish up my required gathered skirt, fashioned from a burgundy paisley cotton, at home. The tricky part was the waistband, which had to be folded over the gathers, which were themselves another tricky part. It fastened with a hook and eye, sewn by hand. I'm pretty sure I never wore the skirt, unless perhaps we were required to wear it to school one day.

Anyway, when sewing with that old machine or my newish one, I have discovered that if you read the manual and follow the directions you can figure out a lot of things. Understand? I'll say it again: If you read the manual and follow the directions, you can figure out a lot of things. A major problem in life is not believing that this is true. These are hard-won lessons, from me to you.

Some years after abandoning that Kenmore on the lawn, I noticed that the seams of our yellow pillowcases, a wedding gift, had ripped. I realized how easily a machine could fix a simple seam in a jiffy. I spied a basic Singer Simplicity machine at Joann's and mulled over the purchase for a few months, remembering the trauma and horror of trying to manage the old machine, but eventually went for it.

This machine presents many of the familiar problems—thread breaking, fabric puckering, machine jamming. It's working better now, though, since I braved the coronavirus to cart it to a small sewing shop for service. The young man in charge was cheerfully scornful of my primitive little Singer. "All plastic!" he shouted repeatedly, insisting it wasn't worth servicing. "You can't oil plastic!" Amidst the exclamations, he changed the needle, dusted the innards, and oiled the metal bobbin mechanism. The humble little "guy," as he kept calling the machine, now works like a dream. Which takes us directly to D.

D Is for Dog

AS YOU READ IN THE PRECEDING CHAPTER, I'M FINISHING up D before C because of the way the pages are laid out. Don't even ask. It will take me until near the end of the entire project to comprehend how the pages are assembled.

Our D comes from the Greek letter *delta* (Δ) and seems to derive from a hieroglyph representing the door of a tent; it's shaped like a triangle. A bird's eye view of the mouth of a river forms a triangle of sand, which gave us our word *delta*, as in the Mississippi Delta. It also has lent its name to a nasty genetic variant of the coronavirus.

The dog gives me a great deal of trouble, and I'm trying not to resent him. (He looks like a boy dog to me. Notice I call the cat "she.") This is too bad because your whole family likes dogs. Grandpa likes dogs, I like dogs, and your dad likes dogs. Your mom loves dogs so much that she exacted a wedding vow from your dad that they could adopt a dog. That's right, one of their actual vows was that she could have a dog sometime when circumstances allowed. Also, she vowed to cook once a month. She hasn't quite fulfilled that vow, just as your dad hasn't (at this moment) fulfilled the dog one. They recently wrangled permission from the landlady of their Brooklyn apartment, Coco Fusco (a pretty famous artist—look her up), that they could have a dog. But that was right before they found out you two were on their way. The dog is now postponed indefinitely.

•

You may remember or at least have heard tell of your parents' friends' dog Bella. Her name is pronounced the Spanish way, Bay-uh, because her owner,

Alicia, is Salvadoran. Bella, a memorable character, is vertically challenged. She has a long bulky body on short legs, like a coffee table. Her appearance is unusual, not to say comical.

So is her personality. She picks up her food dish and carries it around the house, hoping someone will absentmindedly drop a snack in it. Sometimes she plants herself in front of any available human, the food dish in her mouth á la Snoopy, looking beseeching and pathetic. Your mom sent me a video of Bella gingerly walking up the stairs holding her full dish perfectly level and not spilling a kibble.

Dogs generally love to eat, but Bella is surpassingly food-obsessed. During 2018's Christmas season, her limitless appetite necessitated an emergency trip to the vet. Your parents and her owners came home from an evening out and upon greeting Bella perceived a minty fragrance. Sure enough, little bits of peppermint were sticking to her face. Tracing the clues backward, they discovered that she had snagged an unopened, plastic-wrapped tin of Trader Joe's peppermint chocolate bark from a table. Bella chewed off the plastic and, more amazingly, worked the tin open. Then she devoured the contents.

Because chocolate can poison dogs, the humans observed Bella carefully. At first, she seemed fine. But then she seemed a little logy. They didn't know if she merely had an upset tummy or if she was deathly ill. They rushed her to a veterinary emergency room, where her stomach was pumped—at the cost of $1200 for one holiday indulgence.

That same year your mom and dad were coming to our house for the holidays. They alternate traveling to Nashville to see your other grandparents and to visit us in Cleveland year by year. Bella's mom and dad were traveling to Canada for the holiday, so Bella came to Cleveland for Christmas. You can imagine how vigilant I was—the entire family was—to keep food away from Bella. There's often a lot of chocolate at our house around Christmastime, and we couldn't relax unless we put it on top of the refrigerator. Even then we kept our eyes on Bella.

I hope you remember our little dog Roxie, but I suspect you probably won't. Dogs' lives are entirely too short. Roxie, an eight-pound Maltese mix, was not a gracious hostess to Bella. Friendly Bella greets everyone joyously, human or canine. Roxie was reserved and nervous about having another dog in the house, especially one so much bigger and so rambunctious. Bella wanted to play, and Roxie did not. Bella would chase Roxie, which terrified little Roxie, outweighed by at least forty pounds. Around about the house they ran, until someone called off Bella or grabbed Roxie out of harm's way (as she saw it).

Your other grandparents love dogs as well. They have, as I write, a chihuahua named DC. Your great-grandad owned her sister Trixie, and since his death a couple of years ago, both dogs live with your Nashville grandparents. Pop loved that dog. They were best friends.

Our fabric D dog is not such a friend to me. I am not careful enough when cutting out the ears to begin with; they look a little messy, and I'm afraid they're going to unravel. The stitching around the face and eyes looks untidy too. The nose tilts oddly, and I apply the muzzle crookedly. I like the smile, however, and the D itself looks mighty fine. I have made further use of the pawprint fabric.

Grandpa's family owned many dogs. Sparkle Plenty, named for a beautiful little girl in the old Dick Tracy comic strip, had a memorable nervous habit of peeing in the house, so much so that our friend Frank suggested that she would have been better named Sprinkle Plenty. Cindy, an intelligent and calm black cocker spaniel, was the most beloved Ewing dog. All these predated me. I entered the family in the era of Simone, a floppy sheepdog. In fact, the first time I entered the Ewing home, Aunt Barbara was in the midst of giving a birthday party for Simone, who was waiting alone downstairs in the rec room while Barbara gathered her friends upstairs, all adorned in party hats. Barbara opened the door to let Simone upstairs, and everyone shouted "Surprise!"

Regarding Aunt Barbara's throwing a surprise party for a dog, her brother, your grandpa, commented to me, "And people think I'm the eccentric one."

The most beloved of my childhood dogs, contemporaneous with Gray Girl, was Abbie. A smallish black-and-white cocker mix, she was an intelligent, undemanding dog whose sole eccentricity was that she liked climbing trees. She'd walk backwards to the middle of our front yard, her eyes fixed on the willow tree. Then she'd run straight up the trunk to reach me, waiting for her on the lowest branch. She could leap up on a branch of the maple tree on the corner of our lot and cuddle next to me as we looked out over the street below us. As a child, I often wanted to be out of the way, to escape complicated, emotional, adult goings-on inside our house. Abbie and the trees provided a haven: cool shade, a breeze rustling the leaves, and a sweet, uncomplicated dog.

I hope your alphabet dog presages many loving canine relationships in your future.

E Is for Envelope

E is English's favorite letter. This popularity will probably increase, as Michael Rosen points out in *Alphabetical: How Every Letter Tells a Story*, because of e-mails and e-commerce and e-shopping and other words preceded by electronic. Rosen also cites our past tense "-ed" and our frequent plural "-es", as well as the ubiquitous *the*. All of these uses explain why a Scrabble game has twelve Es in contrast to the pathetically underused U, which numbers only four. Your grandpa will hardly ever play Scrabble with me because he insists that I always win, but our scorecards tell a different story. (He wins plenty.) My Scrabble-playing dates back to childhood; my parents were formidable wordsmiths. My mom behaved unpleasantly if you played your letters on a space she had her eye on, sighing and shaking her head. But not as unpleasantly as when my bridge skills disappointed her, which means I gave up bridge but continue playing Scrabble.

The Greeks gave E the elegant name *epsilon* (E), which means "bare" or "essential," because it was its own sound and was not combined in a diphthong. The letter's pictographic history shows that it began as a human figure with arms upraised, signifying joy. This concept may have related to the Semitic word *he*, a word like yay! or hurrah! Like other letters, it flipped sideways, and its shape simplified into a vertical line with the head and arms—three horizontal lines—sticking out to the right.

The E page requires sewing a fabric envelope and attaching it to the page. I use the white holiday fabric with the snowflakes that I mentioned earlier and some dotted Swiss navy-blue fabric. I add a red heart appliqué. The E is easy enough (E is for *easy*); right angles are a snap to cut and to sew. The pattern instructions suggest that you tuck a photo or a love note addressed to Baby into the fabric envelope. I decide to create a cross-stitch note saying *love* because I like cross stitch, and I have fun finding a pattern for the letters and flowers, and choosing the colors. I fuse the dotted Swiss fabric onto the back page using fusible webbing. Thus I learn a trick I might make use of in the future. I can make little fabric envelopes for gift cards or other gifts. I must reread the instructions carefully because spatial relation tasks involving folding and turning things inside out do not come easily to me.

I sometimes make envelopes out of paper too. My friend Chris inspired me in this, along with many other craft activities. In fact, she created a fabric alphabet book for a baby we knew many years ago, which motivated me to attempt yours. Like her, I sometimes send homemade cards to people. Mine are vastly inferior to her meticulous, stylish ones. Mine always look as though I didn't measure carefully because generally I don't measure carefully. Because a homemade card may not be a standard size, you must design a bespoke envelope. I use an online instructional video to remind myself how to do it. This stratagem also works when you have an unusual-size, store-bought card whose envelope has disappeared.

Just as these tasks make me think of Chris, they help me think about you as well because I imagine you perusing the alphabet book. For now, I'm moved by imagining you living your aquatic lives in utero.

Though you're still nebulous to me, I talk about you on the rare occasions that I go out. You become more real when I attend a memorial reception (outdoors in a backyard, everyone in masks) and tell some friends about you and the alphabet book. "You'll have to make two of them!" a mother of twins tells me. (These twins, a boy and a girl, are high school friends of your mom.) She suggests what I have already planned on: to make a numbers book. Now that I know the techniques, I can probably wing it without a pattern.

Speaking of that outdoor memorial reception, I learned that a friend, a member of my book group, has caught the coronavirus. She can't smell or taste, has a cough and fever, and aches all over. She took a COVID test after being sick for more than a week. She couldn't acquire a test any sooner because they were in high demand before the Thanksgiving holiday. President Trump announced months ago that anyone who wants a test for the virus can have one, but that has never been true. She thinks she caught the virus at that outdoor reception for our mutual friend Jeanne. She recently turned seventy-five, and her husband is over eighty, so it's a worry. So much for feeling safe outdoors.

It occurs to me that an elephant more commonly represents the letter E. Your mom and dad actually have some connections to elephants. They traveled to Thailand for their honeymoon in 2016 and stayed at the Elephant Nature Park, a sanctuary founded by a formidable woman named Sangduen "Lek" (Thai for "small") Chailert. They sent lovely pictures of your mom petting a friendly elephant and a video of a mother elephant pulling her baby back from a fence. Ask them about this trip when you're old enough.

E also suggests exercise. Beginning when your mom was about three, I began exercising with my friend and neighbor Tricia. She had sent in a Kimberly-Clark proof of purchase to receive a Low-Impact Aerobic Program video, produced for the American Heart Association and narrated by "Toni Beck of the Spa at the Crescent in Dallas, Texas," a phrase we memorized from hearing it almost every day. For eight years or so we met several times a week in her living room, often with our friends Teresa and Cynthia. While we lunged and swung and stretched along with our limber leaders, Jim and Sherry, we discussed the candidacies of Michael Dukakis and Bill Clinton, Operation Desert Storm, and the fictional travails of Michael and Hope on the TV show *Thirtysomething*. When we began, around 1988, your mom and Tricia's younger son, Eric, were little enough to crawl around underneath us or climb on top of us when we were lying down.

Your mom turned into an actual athlete, playing softball and field hockey and joining the renowned Swim Cadets, synchronized swimmers, at Heights High. I like to think she started thinking about fitness when exercising with her mom. She's maintained her exercise regimen much better than I, however.

When we wanted a challenge, Tricia pulled out her Kathy Smith tape. Kathy Smith presented an unreasonable body image, literally resembling a human Barbie doll. She wore cute workout clothes, which your mom liked. Because she was smitten with the statuesque Ms. Smith, we bought a couple of videotapes as gifts. When your mom turned five, she celebrated with an aerobics birthday party.

After some preliminary games at that soirée, your mom disappeared upstairs to slip into her svelte black leotard. She returned to line up her friends in front of the TV and signaled to me to start the Kathy Smith tape. Everyone tried to follow, they really did. Of course, your mom had practiced the routine before and knew when to swing her arms and when to step to the left and right. Because the little guests had never seen the tape before and maybe because they were not as passionate about aerobics as your mom, and also were encumbered by party dresses and patent-leather shoes, they lagged behind, bumped into each other, fell down, and giggled. Off and on, they turned their attention elsewhere. Your mom pleaded and then scolded, and when those girls wouldn't settle down, she began yelling. As so often happens at kids' parties, the birthday girl had to be escorted upstairs until she could compose herself.

This is the little girl who grew up to be a school teacher. Now under strict control of her emotions, she reinvents a school for reopening during a pandemic, directing students up one stairway and down another. She's a soon-to-be mother with dozens of Kon Mari-ed hand-me-down onesies folded and labeled in a dresser drawer. She still likes to manage. She still likes to organize. You two—with your toys, clothes, future school supplies, and myriad activities—will put her natural gifts to the test.

F Is for Frog

MANY FROGS ARE NO MORE GREEN THAN IS AN OCTOPUS
(See O.) Even so, we associate the color green with frogs despite the reality of their drabness. I'm reminded of a passage in one of my favorite books, Annie Dillard's *Pilgrim at Tinker Creek.* The chapter is called "Seeing."

> My eyes account for less than one percent of the weight of my head; I'm bony and dense; I see what I expect. I once spent a full three minutes looking at a bull-frog that was so unexpectedly large I couldn't see it even though a dozen enthusiastic campers were shouting directions. Finally, I asked, "What color am I looking for?" and a fellow said, "Green." When at last I picked out the frog, I saw what painters are up against: the thing wasn't green at all, but the color of wet hickory bark.

Of course, some tropical frogs are a luminescent green. The rainforest's red-eyed tree frog, for example, is a brilliant lime green. Kermit, the most famous frog of them all, sang a famous song about his challenging skin tone, but frogs we might see in Ohio or where you live in New York City are more of the wet hickory bark variety. For a cartoony, children's book frog, green is the ticket.

Frog, in case you were wondering, is not Latinate. It's from the Germanic *frogga*. The Latin word for *frog* was *rana*, and a little frog was a *ranunculus*. *Rana* gives its name to a genus of many frog species and became the Spanish word for *frog*. We'll have to trust the linguists that the French word *grenouille* derives ultimately from *rana* as well. Interestingly, *frog* is also a derogatory word for a French person, presumably because they start with the same two letters and frog legs are a specialty of French cuisine.

The letter F was a lot of things in its history. Its Phoenician ancestor was a vowel for a while and then began sounding like a W. Its Greek ancestor, *digamma* (F), gradually disappeared for lack of use. After such a long, counter-intuitive evolution, F has ended up as the letter we know: the voiceless labiodental fricative. These marvelously polysyllabic words mean it's not voiced (unlike V), the teeth touch the lip (labiodental), and it emits air (fricative.)

•

I was about to say that we used to have pet frogs in our house, but they were actually toads. Nowadays, I would not allow the capture of wild animals, but before I was enlightened, the kids snagged them when they were visiting a park with our neighbor Peter and his dad, Joe. They named them Mindy and Terry, and the toads lived for at least a few months in a box in our kitchen. They were not green but rather reminiscent of wet hickory bark. We bought them mealworms at the pet store. When they could see the worms moving, they would dart after them faster than you could see them move.

I'm way too soft-hearted now; it's hard for me to imagine that I let the kids keep wild toads in our kitchen and sacrificed live mealworms to them. I wasn't a vegetarian then, for one thing. In general, I'm much less able now to tolerate death and suffering, normal though they may be, in the animal kingdom, movies, TV, books, and the news. And I feel sad that Mindy and Terry were removed from their natural homes. None of us knew better then.

On a more cheerful note, Mindy and Terry evoke the customary cuteness of kids' names for pets. We like to recall that our friends and neighbors, the Janors, had cats named Snowball and Florian. Our own long-lived goldfish were named Goldie and Freddy. Those guys lived for years, sustained by my careful cleaning of their bowl and infrequent feedings. Your mom, desperate for pets, adopted a hermit crab for a while and named him or her Henree. Presumably, the whimsical spelling made the name appropriate for any gender. It's a sad memory now, because when Henree died, we couldn't be sure. Because hermit crabs aren't particularly ambulatory, we let the corpse sit for a week or so to make sure.

Your mom at last insisted we leave amphibians and mollusks behind and acquire ourselves an actual canine. She begged relentlessly. Grandpa and I weren't averse to the idea. We were just very good at procrastinating. But you know your mom. She's dogged, so to speak. All that year, 1995, she harped on getting a dog. Then one fall evening, your great-aunt Marge found a box of puppies by the side of the road, Gladys and her Pips, and we happened to be traveling to her farm in Minerva for Thanksgiving.

Without telling your mom or Uncle Doug, Grandpa and I conspired to pick out a puppy and bring it home. We kept this plan a secret from the smaller humans in our family.

Arriving at the farm before dark, we trekked out to the cozy barn, said hello to the horses, and paid a visit to the wriggling boxful of puppies. That's how Marge had found them, several weeks before. She and Ed were driving on a dark country road not far from their farm when their headlights caught something moving on the berm. Marge told Ed to stop the car, and he rested his forehead on the steering wheel and said something like, "Oh, boy. Here we go." They backed up and saw that some of the puppies, or at least the adventurous little black one, had scooched out of the box and was about to climb onto the road. Of course, they put them in the car! Of course, they brought them home!

We focused on the three males, because Marge had already claimed Gladys. The one with scruffy brindle fur became Scruff, adopted by one of Marge's friends. The particularly wiggly one with a sleek black coat was chosen by your cousin Stephanie. She and her musician husband, Tim, a guitarist, named the puppy Mingus, after the revered jazz bassist and pianist. Your mom and Doug sat entranced on the dirt floor while the puppies greeted them deliriously. A particularly sweet ball of fuzzy fur approached hesitantly. Marge described his modest demeanor as "aw, shucks." After several minutes of oohing and ahhing, we told your mom and Doug we could bring him home, to unrestrained joy and jubilation. Marge lent us a carrier, and on the drive home he sat between the kids on the backseat while we discussed his name. Grandpa said he liked Marge's description. "How about Shucks?" he said. Shucks it was, as you have seen.

I remember a few weeks later trying to teach an exasperating Sunday school class in which your smitten mom wouldn't stop telling the other kids about her new puppy. We were discussing, I remember, the Beatitudes. Your mom was laboring to connect each Beatitude to Shucks, annoying me no end with her interruptions. When we reached "The meek will inherit the earth," one of the kids asked, "What is 'meek'?" Heather, my fellow teacher, explained that meek means quiet and gentle and peaceful. Margaret quipped, "My new puppy is meek!" which was in this case actually true. My wise friend Heather said, "I'm sure he is. And what does that do for him? Does that make you love him more?" Your mom, taken aback at the genuine lesson being offered, said that it did.

Shucks the Meek lived for about sixteen years, long after your mom went to Syracuse University, graduated, and moved to New York. A lot of comings and goings. Christmas and summers and leaving again on trips. I wrote this poem about one of their farewells.

Girl Going to College: Saying Goodbye to the Dog

Her face is an inch away
as you doze,
the girl who was here when you arrived as a puppy.
She was little then, and would run.
Big now, she peers at your face,
trying to figure you out one last time.
You lie still, snoozing. She strokes your soft ear,
your muzzle, places her lips against the side of your head.
She is solemn,
contemplating, for a moment, the break she's soon to make,
leaving you behind with your two old caretakers.
She rests her forehead on yours,
while you sleep on, as you do most days, all day,
dreaming of a little girl.

G Is for Giraffe

I BEGIN WORKING ON THE GIRAFFE PAGE SOON AFTER THE dog debacle. My hopes are not high. Same fabric, same thread, and most ominously, same curves and turns. To my surprise, though, the stitching goes smoothly! The face and tail cause me a little consternation, however. I could draw them with a fabric pen, as the instructions suggest, but because I can embroider, I feel I should embroider. Alas, among the myriad colors in my box, there is no brown floss.

I make a fraught trip to Walmart, which I confess to visiting several times in the course of this project. I normally boycott Walmart, only about five minutes from my house, because of their predatory retail practices. Some twenty-five years ago, I served on a committee to prevent Walmart from coming to our city, and at that time we succeeded. But they weaseled their way back and settled in at Severance Towne Center in our town of Cleveland Heights. It used to be an indoor mall but was renovated into outdoor-facing big-box stores. Then a new development arose on the golf course and sylvan grounds of a beautiful old country club about a mile away. Despite determined community resistance, the retailers had their way, and Walmart left its decaying big box at Severance and moved to its new location where long fairways and beautiful trees used to stand. Now a Walmart superstore is accompanied by TJ Maxx, Burlington Coat Factory, and any number of fast-food places.

I don't generally shop there on principle, and I always have an unhappy experience at checkout. One time, after I waited ten or fifteen minutes in line, the cashier abruptly walked off, leaving us stranded to find another line. I don't blame her. She was probably having an awful day and hated working at Walmart, but it was no fun to wait another fifteen minutes in another line. In addition,

Walmart is often crowded, and crowds are anathema during this pandemic. I am embarrassed to admit to my ultrasafe friends that I entered a Walmart.

Here's the situation. Walmart stocks sewing supplies. Otherwise, I must travel to the nearest Joann's, about twenty minutes east of me. Today I need brown floss to finish the giraffe, some empty bobbins, and some white thread. Yes! I've been sewing so much that I have almost used up my basic white thread! Therefore, I set foot into Walmart, navigating the busy aisles as quickly as I can. I endure a long wait at checkout, keeping my distance from a young man in front of me who tucks his face mask under his lower lip, inscrutably protecting his chin. After such an excursion, I brood over every cough and imagine a constant headache, sure that I'm going to be punished for my foolishness. Such is the time we're enduring.

Anyway, once home, I thread a needle with brown floss. Giraffe's eyes become French knots, and her little smile is a split stitch. I try stitching some horns, but they resemble curved goat's horns. I google to study some actual giraffe horns.

I discover that giraffe horns are called ossicones. The first half of the word derives from os, the Latin word for "bone," as in ossification. Cones is precisely what it sounds like; it's from Latin conus, meaning "cone." That's because of the horns' shape. They're actually made of ossified cartilage, rather than true bone. Baby giraffes have them, but they lie flat against their heads before they're born, out of courtesy to their mothers. Both males and females have them. Males use them during fights with other males, called necking. The ossicones grow heavier with age and sometimes do real damage when giraffes are battling.

The tiny horns on your giraffe are unthreatening, not cone-shaped, and a little crooked. Though I examine pictures before sewing, I am not attempting true authenticity. The tail is a bunch of brown floss knotted and joined. It turns out pretty well.

While googling, I discover that Cleveland Metroparks Zoo has announced the birth of a male giraffe calf. Calf and his mom, Jada, are often visible to guests in the giraffe barn. They are expected to join the rest of the zoo's Masai giraffe herd in the outdoor habitat alongside dad, Bo, nearly two-year-old Zawadi, and his mom, Jhasmin. The calf weighs approximately 101 pounds at birth and stands about six feet tall. You will each be something less than one-tenth of that weight when you are born. While the calf has been observed nursing and bonding with mom, he is considered small compared to typical male giraffe calves that can weigh about 150 pounds at birth. Cleveland Metroparks Zoo veterinarians and animal care teams have been monitoring him closely. Giraffes can live as long as forty years in captivity. Maybe someday we will visit Jada and her family at the Cleveland Metroparks Zoo.

Like ossicones, the letter G has an ancient history. In our C chapter, we met its ancestor, an Egyptian hieroglyph meaning "throwing stick" or "boomerang."

The Greek letter *gamma* was shaped like an upside-down capital L (Γ). It had a right angle rather than a curve. The Romans turned the *gamma* into roughly the shape we now have. The Romans used it for the hard G sound, as in *goat*, but for us it can also represent the soft sound of *Georgia*. It also sounds like "zh," especially in words we borrow from French, such as the ending of *garage*. In many words, it makes no sound at all, like *gnu*, *light*, and *weigh*. Why so many sounds for one letter? Michael Rosen in his book about the alphabet explains wryly, "The main reason for all this is to make children (and people for whom English is an additional language) cross, unhappy, or both."

So much of English spelling is similarly crazy, in that it doesn't represent English sounds consistently. Contemplate *cellophane*, for example. That C at the beginning could sound like K (calico) or CH (cello) or S (cellophane). Attributing an F sound to PH is not normal English phonetics but derives from ancient Greek. The A can have any number of phonic permutations (father, cat, lane), and the E at the end is a complete waste of ink. This redundancy is why Ben Franklin promoted a shorter, more phonetic alphabet.

To illustrate the seeming randomness of English spelling, you may someday run across this example: *ghoti* spells *fish*. How? The GH in *enough* sounds like an F. The O in *women* sounds like a short I. Finally, TI makes the SH sound in words such as *motion* and *nation*. I always believed that the English playwright George Bernard Shaw created this word to criticize the vagaries of English spelling. My recent research proves me wrong. *Ghoti* appears nowhere in Shaw's writing, though I have attributed it to him countless times in my teaching.

Instead *ghoti* comes from an 1855 letter by English publisher Charles Ollier, who attributes the coinage to his son, who, like Shaw, enjoyed ridiculing nonsensical English spelling.

•

As a soon-to-be grandma who's thinking about G, I've been reflecting on grandmothers, both my own and your mom's. Grandma Grimm (two Gs!) was my mom's mom. She lived near us in Louisville, Ohio, where she had moved from Cleveland when my oldest sister Betsey was born. (Grandparents long to be near their grandchildren.) In many ways a stereotypical grandma, she hugged you hard, jamming your face against the jeweled brooches she often wore on her dresses. Always dresses back then; even my mom always wore a dress. Grrandma Grimm visited the hairdresser about once a month and often wore a hairnet to hold the coif in place. An Irish immigrant, she baked soda bread and yeasty dinner rolls. Marge grew frustrated when she tried to write down Grandma's recipes as she baked. She threw in a handful of this and a few pinches of that—no way for us to reproduce those pastries! She baked chicken until the meat melted off the bone.

She never learned to drive but called out, "Jesus, Mary, and Joseph!" when she thought my grandfather, whom we called Pop, took too sharp a turn. She dangled a rosary from her hands in the car as well as during Mass. She kept a neat house and washed her clothes in a ringer washer, which seemed ancient even to us. She had only a seventh-grade education but had worked at a Cleveland specialty food store called Chandler and Rudd. She was, I'm sure, a canny and dependable employee. Her sometime ignorance drove my mom crazy. For example, she disparaged almost all ethnicities aside from the Irish, though she made notable exceptions for American Indians and Jews, for some reason. Somehow sins of bigotry seem more tolerable in a grandparent, though they shouldn't have been.

I didn't know my other grandmother, my dad's mom, who gave me her name. Katharine Brainard Miller was a New Englander and was, I've gathered, somewhat austere. She taught Latin and Greek before her marriage, so I've inherited that, at least the Latin part, as well. She lived with our family for a short while when I was very little. I have one distinct memory of climbing the stairs behind her, noticing that only the soles of her shoes touched the steps, not the chunky heels. I was only about four when she died, so this memory may not be real, but its odd specificity lends it credibility.

Your mom's grandmothers were distinctly different from each other. Grandma Miller, my mom, was, as I say elsewhere, so difficult a person that I wrote a book about her. Over many years, I've realized more about your great-grandmother. I've thought in the past that she didn't truly love her children or grandchildren. She certainly had trouble showing love. But now I think that while her feelings were as strong as any mother's, she suffered from a disability that short-circuited her emotions. Her feelings twisted inside her like a knotted rope. Parental love is scary in its power. My mother hid hers behind bitterness and depression, and that was a sad loss, sadder even for her than for children and grandchildren.

When your mom and Doug came to her nursing home with me, she'd smile at them vaguely and utter platitudes but never ask them questions. Often a big box of chocolates from Heggy's, a Canton institution, would be sitting on her dresser. When the kids were clearly bored and restless, I'd ask if they could have a piece of candy. "Of course," she'd say, but she never thought to offer them herself. I can't help thinking about her now. I check my phone often to see if I've heard from your mom. I look forward to your birth and grieve in advance that I can't be present and that the pandemic will force me to stay home for a while after you're born. I talk to your mom after her doctor appointments and peruse the ultrasound pictures she sends. All these are normal behaviors. In contrast, my mom never asked a question I can recall during my pregnancies, and though we called to tell her your mom had been born, she never called us back in the weeks following. She just didn't make phone calls. She telephoned me perhaps a half dozen times in my whole life. She died when your mom was nine, but I doubt that your mom has much memory of her, though we didn't live far away and saw her fairly often.

Grandma Ewing, your grandpa's mother, never stopped asking questions, especially when I was pregnant. She suggested the name Marietta, a name she had always liked. She often mused beforehand that your mom would be born with blue eyes and a full head of dark hair, which turned out to be true. When Uncle Doug and your mom were born, Grandma Ewing nagged us to let her babysit. She loved shopping and bought your mom quilted dresses and dresses with appliqués and flocking and ruffles. I've always thought that's where your mom acquired her fashion sense. Not from me, surely.

On December 5, 1993, Grandma and Poppie Ewing drove about an hour from Canton to watch your mom, then seven years old, perform in the ice show at the Cleveland Heights Recreation Pavilion. Your mom was quite the little skater and performed in several numbers in the chorus. The graceful older girls she idolized had solo parts. They skated to music from *A Chorus Line*, *Phantom of the Opera*, and *Cats*—music right up Grandma Ewing's alley; she loved musicals. Your mom's age group skated to songs from *Annie*. After the show, Grandma asked your mom how the previous two nights had gone and wanted to know all about the other skaters and songs.

Grandma and Poppie sat with us way up in the stands. I was aware during the show that my mother-in-law's poor vision made it unlikely that she was seeing much. Afterward, she shared a story about herself. Grandma and Poppie had been to some performance a night or two before, maybe *The Nutcracker*. At some point she had to leave her seat in the dark and almost lost her balance. She leaned on the shoulder of the woman in front of her to steady herself and then realized her hand was firmly attached to the woman's head, not her shoulder! It was the kind of story she was always telling on herself and laughing about.

Later that evening the kids and I were going caroling, and Grandpa went off to dinner with his parents. He told me later that they had had a nice time.

The next evening, Uncle David called us to say that Grandma Ewing had been taken to the hospital. Apparently, after a holiday party, she had been straightening a decoration on her Christmas tree when Poppie found her lying on the living room floor. She died of an apparent heart attack. She was only seventy.

It makes me sad that your mom doesn't clearly remember Grandma Ewing, who loved her so much and so well. Your mom's middle name, Darr, comes from Grandma Ewing's maiden name. She was an excellent, loving, attentive grandmother. She is my grandmother role model.

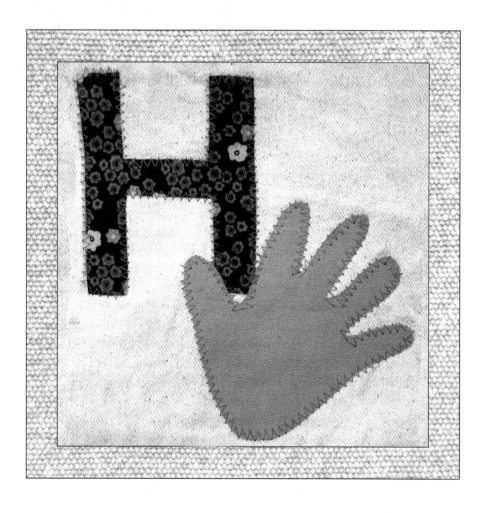

H Is for Hand

THE SEVENTH LETTER OF THE GREEK ALPHABET, CALLED *eta*, was pronounced like our letter H. Its Semitic progenitor was named *cheth*, borrowing an Egyptian hieroglyph that looks like a chain of twisted rope. That shape simplified itself into the Greek capital H, which was passed on to the Romans and then to us. It creates more controversy than most of its alphabetical siblings, especially in Great Britain, where people can be judged, à la the musical *My Fair Lady*, for dropping their Hs. A lower-class Briton might say "'orse" for "horse" and thereby reveal 'is or 'er class and level of education. On the other hand, H is often supposed to be silent, especially for English words derived from the French, such as honor. Why then should people be criticized for occasionally dropping their "'aitches"?

Reading about these disputes reminds me of a linguistic question that's long bugged me, especially since I've been at home during the pandemic perusing YouTube videos. Why does true-blue American Martha Stewart aspirate the first letter of *herb* as the Brits do rather than leaving it silent as we simple folk do? Turns out the Internet contains a fair amount of discussion on this point, the upshot of which is that Martha aspires to sound British. Or at least she's guilty of hypercorrection, an effort to sound correct by applying a rule (aspirating the H) where it doesn't apply. Hypercorrection is trying too hard to follow the rule you imagine applies and thereby breaking the actual rule. Using *whom* in all contexts and *I* as an object (Mother called Ralph and I) are hypercorrections in vogue right now.

Sometimes I'm tempted to expatiate about the alphabet's letter and such language matters when I don't have much to say about the pictured object—a hand, in this case. In this book—the adult book you're reading now, not the

49

alphabet book—I set myself the task of writing about every letter and every object associated with it. For many letters, that presents no problem; I have plenty to say about cats and dogs, for example, as you've seen. But rockets and yoyos? Not so much.

The fabric page itself is easy enough. Even the curves of the fingers are easy to sew around, and stitching around an H can't be easier: all straight lines and right angles. I use plain teal fabric for the hand itself and the brown and teal print that appears on the cover for the letter. Smooth sewing while you're making it, but no rough patches to write about later. There's not much point in writing about projects that go smoothly.

Writing about *hand*, on the other hand, is vexing me, until, at last, one frigid January day I go for a walk. We're not supposed to go anywhere except the grocery store, and you can't do that every day. Taking walks allows you to escape the house regardless of the weather. When my hands grew cold that day, it came to me: I have something to say about hands after all!

I used to lie down with your mom when she was little to help her sleep. Her crib was against one wall, and against another wall was the double bed she eventually moved into. Grandpa or I could lie down quietly on the bed and sing or talk to her in her crib. When she moved into the big double bed, she still wanted me to lie down beside her after we had read a book. Doug was usually with us for reading, and then I tucked him in his own bed and returned to your mom. This lying-down habit came to present a bit of a problem because your mom would wake when I stirred, or she'd wake after I was relaxing downstairs. I'd hear her crying. This was when she was very little, up until she was eight or nine.

I say it was a problem, but I mean that it was a problem at the time. Now I think: what was so important that I had to do? The dishes couldn't wait? What work was so urgent, or what TV show could I not miss? To think I would leave your mom to watch *Cheers*, now that she's grown up and lives far away, seems unimaginable. Of course, when your kids are small, you have so many other things to do, and there are things you want to do, like read or watch TV. You may even wickedly wish time to pass so that the kids would grow up. But now I would give anything to return to an hour lying down and whispering to your mom in that soft bed. Anyway, I was recalling those evenings as my hands grew cold on that walk.

Even indoors, my hands are often cold. When forced to shake hands with someone (not now during this pandemic and maybe never again), I often apologize before our hands meet. Sorry about my cold hands! And the other person usually says, "That's okay!" or "Cold hands, warm heart," even when my chilliness has made them jump. The sign of peace at Mass is socially challenging for me from about October to April for this reason.

But when she was little your mom liked my cold hands; I guess because when you're little you really like your mom. My cold hands were part of me, and so she liked them. Even lying in the bed next to her, my hands would often be cold, and your mom would grasp my icy index finger and rub it gently against her lips and face. We'd talk about our day, and I'd respond to her questions.

She asked good questions. When Grandma Ewing died, your mom was only seven. Her cousins scared her by saying that Grandma had become a ghost, which even now makes me a little mad. We would lie together talking about how much Grandma loved her. I would assure your mom that even if Grandma Ewing were a ghost, she'd be a gentle and loving one.

We would talk about her nursery school class. At first she felt shy around her teacher, Mrs. Gall. Mrs. Gall sang a hello song every day in which she said hello to each child, and the child was supposed to respond, "Fine, thank you. How are you?" Lying in bed, your mom told me she really liked Mrs. Gall. When I asked why, she said it was because if she didn't answer the song, Mrs. Gall sang it for her.

Before going downstairs, I would tell your mom I loved her, and she would reply something like, "I love you how big the house is." With her clinging to my cold hand, we'd go back and forth, one-upping each other. I love you how big the house is. I love you how big the country is. I love you how big the world is. I love you how big the universe is.

That's how much I still love your mom. It's how much your mom loved you when you were small and how much she still loves you. How big the universe is. That's how much.

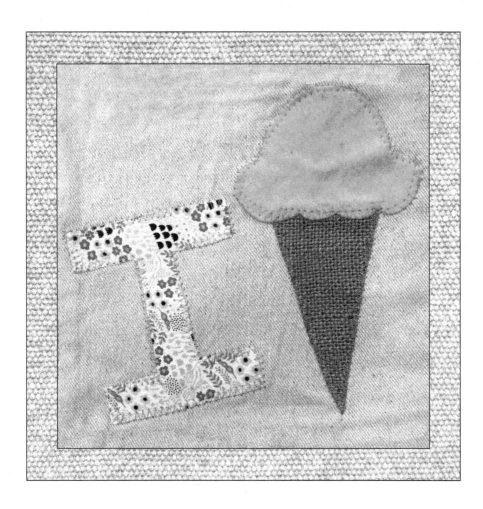

I Is for Ice Cream

WHEN WE WERE FIRST MARRIED, YOUR GRANDFATHER AND I lived a few blocks north of Taggart's Ice Cream Parlor on Fulton Road in Canton. We strolled down the wide, tree-lined street to Taggart's regularly on summer evenings, and before we were married your grandfather rented an apartment in an old house right next door. Taggart's, a solid brick building with big maple booths and marble counters, successfully appears old-timey, because it is. They serve soup and sandwiches, but ice cream is their thing, and their special confection is the Bittner, a large, thick chocolate shake topped with roasted salted pecans. When there's no pandemic and I show friends around Canton, I take them to Taggart's.

Though we have been buying ice cream together for over forty years, your grandfather recently opined that my favorite flavor is butter pecan. All these years, I have never ordered butter pecan. Not at Taggart's. Not at the Incredible Scoop, a former neighborhood Cleveland Heights spot where we used to take your mom. Not at Mitchell's, a Cleveland institution. Not at our nearby Ben and Jerry's or United Dairy Farmers. Even so, he returned from a recent errand with my purported favorite—butter pecan. It was my mother's favorite, as well as his dad's, so maybe that's why he was confused. Or maybe the Bittner's pecans confused him.

When your mom and dad visit, or when we visit them in New York, we usually find an opportunity to go out for ice cream. Nobody orders the pink kind, like the fabric ice cream cone on your alphabet book page. I like the look of the pink felt fabric for the scoop of ice cream and the brown burlap for the cake cone it sits on. A multi-colored print makes up the I itself.

I derives from the Greek *iota* (ι), the littlest letter, which gives rise to its meaning a very small thing, as in, "I wouldn't give one iota for butter pecan ice cream." Our word *jot*, meaning "a small amount," comes from *iota* also.

As I'm writing in fits and starts, we have now proceeded into a new year when it's ice cold outside and more challenging to go for walks or step out for ice cream. The election has passed and many concomitant events, all I-related, have ensued. As of January 6, 2021, the letter I stands for *insurrection*. We're getting ahead of ourselves because I write more about the election later in the alphabet, under V, but it's not my fault insurrection starts with an I.

Everyone felt very relieved to escape 2020, with its lockdowns, fraught election, unemployment, illness, and horrific racial violence. We had finally turned the corner, when pro-Donald Trump demonstrators descended on Washington, DC, on the day that Congress was to count the electoral college votes, a normally uneventful ritual that would definitively declare Joe Biden the president-elect. Trump and his minions had been denying Biden's win for weeks. Trump rallied with his supporters down the street, along with his sometime lawyer Rudy Giuliani, his smarmy sons, and demagogic Congressman Mo Brooks. They whipped up the crowd, who didn't need whipping up, and many of them headed to the Capitol where Congress was in session. A few hundred stormed the building.

I was watching the Congressional proceedings on TV because it was a momentous day, destined to end (we thought) all the agonizing questioning of the election. Grandpa watched off and on with me. In real time, our favorite reporters, Lisa Desjardins and Yamiche Alcindor of the *PBS Newshour*, watched men pushing past the outnumbered Capitol police and smashing windows with staffs on which hung American flags. We heard the report of a gunshot in real time, as a protester was killed by a policeman. We watched Ms. Desjardins ducking behind furniture when police snapped "Get down!" and heard her whispering into her microphone. Harrowing as it all was, we later learned that the mayhem was even worse in other parts of the building where attackers chanted, "Hang Mike Pence!" They were actually advocating lynching the vice president! They destroyed furniture, they ransacked offices, and House Speaker Nancy Pelosi was in as much danger as the vice president. The days between the insurrection and Inauguration Day passed anxiously, full of trepidations about further violence.

There followed another nerve-wracking I: impeachment. I watched most of Donald Trump's second impeachment trial on TV. House Manager Jamie Raskin's eloquence moved me to check out a biography of Thomas Paine, about whom I learned a few things. He was born in England! He was a corsetmaker! He helped foment the French Revolution! I didn't read very far, however. A Paine biography is the kind of thing I think I want to read, but it turns out I really don't. Jamie Raskin admires Paine so much that he named his son Tommy after him, and Raskin quoted Paine frequently in his impeachment speeches. Paine's namesake, Tommy Raskin, committed suicide only a week before the insurrection and about five weeks before the impeachment trial. It was wrenching to watch Jamie Raskin hold himself together, though sometimes crying, making the case to convict Donald Trump. Unfortunately, most Republicans disagreed.

At last, another important I arrived: inauguration. Thousands of National Guard troops patrolled the area around the Capitol, but even so everyone worried that more violence was coming. The day went smoothly, and we have a new president now, whose administration you will always know because you were born in it, just as I was born in the Truman administration, and your mom and dad were born under Ronald Reagan. Truman makes me sound and feel very old because I remember President Eisenhower and like to think he was president when I was born, but he wasn't elected until the following year.

Anyway, it's a big relief to have a new president. It seemed, for a while, that the lies and efforts to subvert elections were over, though it turns out our relief was misguided. Anyway, the new president, we hear, loves ice cream. His favorite flavor is chocolate chip.

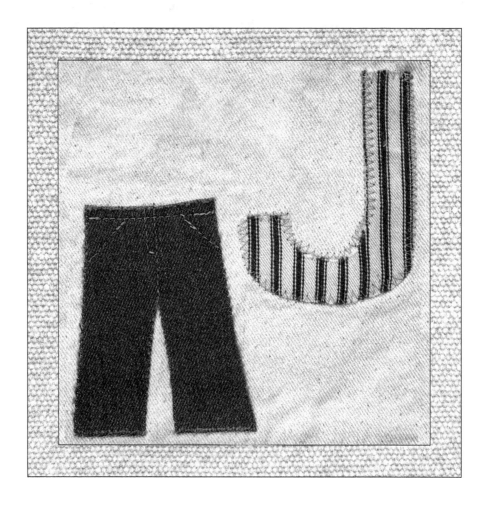

J Is for Jeans

THIS PAGE MAKES ME FEEL CLEVER. BECAUSE I HAVE NO denim remnants, I buy a denim iron-on patch at the store, designed to repair someone's ripped knee. I use the pattern to cut out the jeans shape and iron it onto the page. To enhance the jeans-ness, I add yellow stitching, following pattern directions, and it comes out looking like, well, jeans! Some train conductor's denim striped fabric from long ago, from my mom's house, forms the J.

Jeans themselves have been controversial in my lifetime. They belonged, in my childhood, to farmers or rough kids, like the greasers in SE Hinton's *The Outsiders*. When I was in high school, we were not allowed to wear jeans to school. Girls couldn't wear pants of any kind, in fact. But as soon as I went to college, in 1969, everyone wore jeans all the time. I had a pair of bell bottoms that split at the knees and were patched and torn like the fashionable ripped jeans people wear now. My mom, who usually didn't critique or even notice my clothes, disapproved of my wearing the patched and torn jeans to teach my freshman composition classes when I was a Kent State grad student.

Jeans were a mark of youth and rebellion back then. They gradually sneaked into fashion, so that even Grandpa's mom, Dee, acquired a pair sometime in the early 1980s. They flattered her slim figure, but she gave up wearing them because my more conservative father-in-law, Stan, your great-grandfather, didn't approve. When I was teaching high school in Hartville around the same time, the principal forbade teachers from wearing denim of any sort. Some other teachers thought me quite the scofflaw when I donned my denim jumper and denim skirt for school. I thought his forbidding a fabric was a weird overreach, and the principal never reproached me.

During the quarantine people are once again living in their jeans at home, if, that is, they bother to change out of their pajamas. Facebook posts joke about changing from your daytime pajamas to your nighttime pajamas at the end of the day. Your grandfather never wears jeans but is wearing his least favorite socks, frayed shirts, and torn pants and sweaters every day. Why wear out your good clothes when you're working at home and no one sees you? You might be seen on a Zoom call, but then you're visible only from the chest up. Who cares if you're wearing mustard yellow socks?

The letter J itself is a baby, relative to the rest of the alphabet. Originally, it was a variation on the letter I and was pronounced like our Y. In Latin texts, *Julius* (as in Caesar) is spelled *Iulius*. Words like *juvenile* come from Latin *iuvenis*, meaning "youth" and *janitor* from Ianus, the god of doorways—because the janitor guards the door. In 1524, an Italian scholar named Gian Giorgio Trissino decreed that they should be two separate letters, and so they have been ever since.

Imagining you two babies compels me often to think back on my own babies, your mom and Uncle Doug. That has reminded me of a fond J memory, that is, James Taylor and one of my favorite songs.

James Taylor is one of those cross-generational musicians. My generation's and your mom's taste in popular music overlaps to some extent. As I matured, I liked my parents' big band music pretty well. As an adolescent, I wouldn't have admitted it, and I didn't have the maturity to listen to it on my own. But the millennials genuinely like the Beatles and, by and large, appreciate Motown. Similarly, I still like the music your mom liked when she was in high school—Alanis Morissette (whose Broadway show was canceled by the pandemic—your mom and friends had tickets reserved) and Sarah McLachlan. In July 1997 we saw a traveling music festival of female musicians called Lilith Fair at Blossom Music Center, featuring Ms. McLachlan, Sheryl Crow, Emmylou Harris, Tracy Chapman, Suzanne Vega, and others. We both liked the music.

Your parents' joyous wedding reception incorporated a lot of cross-generational music to please both the young people and the parents in attendance. Your dad didn't dance. He told family members that he and his mom lack the "fun gene." That's not true. He just doesn't dance. But your mom changed from her dress into a sleek white jumpsuit and danced with all her friends and many of their parents. Weeks later, Grandpa told me he started crying when heard a song from the reception on the car radio, "Shut Up and Dance" by Walk the Moon; hearing it caused him to remember the wedding and the dancing.

James Taylor has some history in our household. Your mom and Uncle Doug became infatuated with *New Moon Shine*, his 1991 album, and played it over and over, dancing around the stereo and singing along to "Copperline" and "The Frozen Man." Your other grandmother loves him too. When I visited Nashville in 2015 to help scout out wedding venues, his album *Before This World* was always playing in her car. In 2017, all of us—your parents, Grandma Connie, Grandpa, and I—saw him perform in concert with Bonnie Raitt in our different cities. Your parents sat outside in the rain on Long Island, celebrating their first anniversary. Grandma Connie saw them at Bridgestone Arena in Nashville, and Grandpa and I traveled back to Blossom Music Center for their outdoor concert. Most often, generations and different regions have different tastes, and it's nice to have JT in common.

Back to the special song.

Uncle Doug was mostly an easy baby. He slept well. I always say, to convey his general cooperativeness, that he was born on his due date—June 21, 1982. When I was being wheeled to a room at Canton's Aultman Hospital, the orderly told me that Princess Diana had just gone into labor, and, sure enough, Uncle Doug shares an exact birthday with Prince William, her firstborn. He remained cooperative: later that summer, the night before I had to return to teaching at the end of August, he slept for six hours straight for the first time.

Your mom was by no means a difficult baby, but I'd been spoiled a little by Doug. When she came along, your grandfather worked long hours showing movies, and I spent many evenings home alone with the two of them. After settling Doug for the night (he was three or four at the time I'm speaking of), your mom would often either wake up or had not yet fallen sleep. Like many babies, she had a fussy period as evening fell. She demanded a lot of carrying. When it warmed up outside, I'd walk her in the yard; being outdoors sometimes works magic on fussy babies. She was born in February, though, and we were stuck inside for a month or two. Many evenings, I'd trace a circle around our living room—walking, humming, and cooing. I'd whisper in her ear how lucky I was to have a little girl named Margaret to hold on my shoulder. Even when I was tired and irritable and my back hurt, I meant it.

I took to playing James Taylor's album *That's Why I'm Here* as I walked around and around, which means, of course, a vinyl record on a stereo turntable. I'd move the needle over and over again to my favorite song on the album, "Only a Dream in Rio." The words bear no direct connection to cranky babies, but they convey a mysteriously special time. Appearing on *David Letterman's Late Night*, James Taylor explained the song's genesis. When he toured Brazil, people celebrating the auspicious result of an election inspired the hope-filled song. Random lines felt meaningful to me as I paced around with your mom on my shoulder.

Always during those nights, I realized that I was living a dream, grouchy and overwhelmed though I might have been. I was living a dream with two healthy children in a fortunate middle-class home, healthy, and mostly *compos mentis*. I was walking a warm, dark-haired baby girl around and around the living room. Oh, what a night, wonderful one in a million.

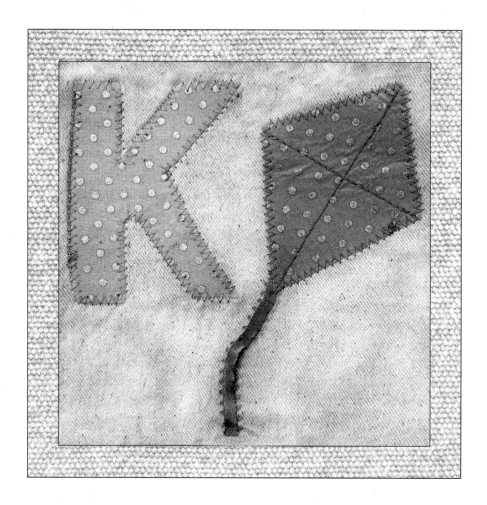

K Is for Kite

THE KITE'S POLKA DOT FABRIC REMAINS FROM SOME PIL-
lowcases I made for your mom and dad's wedding shower in 2016—pink for
her, blue for him. Your book's instructions suggest adding ribbon to the bottom
of the kite. I am hesitant, not sure how it will launder. The fabric book, mauled
and mouthed by babies, is supposed to withstand some washings. I intend to
launder it myself before wrapping it up for your parents. Fingers crossed that it
holds up, ribbon and all.

I rarely flew kites as a kid, and your mom and Doug didn't either. We
never had any luck keeping them aloft. With little to say about kites, I'll
resort to the history of K going back to the Greeks' *kappa* (κ) and back
further to an Egyptian hieroglyph that looks like an outstretched hand.
The Semites called the letter *kaph*, their word for the palm of the hand.
The Greeks turned the upturned fingers to the side and gave it the shape
we now know. K's sound is consistent, except when it's silent, as in *knight*
and *know*. Sometimes it's reinforced with a redundant C, as in the *duck* and
its *quack*.

K begins a lot of our words derived from German: *coffee klatsch*,
Kaiser (which the Germans adapted from Latin *Caesar*), *kitsch*, and *kaput*,
for example. *Kindergarten* is literally German for a *children's garden*, which,
because we homeschooled, your mom did not attend.

A fan of the education writer John Holt and disenchanted with schools'
routines and competition after years of teaching, I decided to keep my kids
home and see how much they could learn. We had lovely long days—reading,
cooking, hanging out, doing crafts, enjoying activities like ice skating, roller
skating, and hiking. We mixed water with cornstarch to form oobleck, which

has weirdly wonderful properties of both liquids and solids. We defrosted the freezer and called it a science project. We attended Wednesday morning story time at our neighborhood library, and afterward your mom arranged books around the living room for an at-home library story hour and allowed Doug and me to check them out. She and Doug played mysterious pretend games with the stuffed animals, enacting plots and creating characters I had no clue about. The two of them sat side by side on the recliner to watch *Sesame Street* at 11:00 AM. We ran errands and carried on lengthy conversations in the car about why salt melted ice and why receiving change at the store was not really about the store giving you money.

To be honest, sometimes Doug and your mom became bored. Sometimes I hid out in the bedroom upstairs because I wanted a break. It helped that we met with other homeschoolers once a week and that your mom and Doug played with the neighborhood kids from late afternoon to dusk every night. From about 1988 to 1999, homeschooling was the salient fact about my life. I had to explain it to bank tellers and store clerks and strangers at parties, and now I rarely think about it.

Though we skipped kindergarten and the grades that followed, your mom did attend nursery school because I hoped it would be innocuous at worst and fun at best. A few days a week for a couple of hours, Doug and I had time to do some math or reading, and your mom—a confident and craft-loving creature—enjoyed nursery school.

Maybe you'll recognize your mom in her four-year-old manifestation. One day her nursery-school class was taking a field trip to the library, and I volunteered to drive. Her friends Dani and Ashley would ride in the car with us. Your mom was excited about the trip, but also felt a heavy burden of responsibility in the planning. She talked all the way to school that morning.

Her primary concern was the seating in the car. If she sat in the front with me (because we weren't yet woke to the dangers of little kids in the front seat), she'd be separated from her friends, which wouldn't be fun. Much better, she decided, for all three girls to sit together in the back. But how to arrange them in the back seat? Who'd sit in the middle? Who'd have the window seats?

As we pulled into the parking lot, your mom came to a decision. "I'll sit in the middle," she said, "because Dani and Ashley will both want to sit next to me." As far as I could tell, the arrangement suited everyone. I don't remember the actual library visit, just that conversation.

When I tell this story, I always add that I never, to this day, would assume that anyone, even my friends, would prefer sitting next to me in any venue. Your mom was sure what Ashley and Dani would want, and she was right.

This conversation also signaled your mom's love of organizing and her attention to detail, evident today in her teaching and her meticulous preparations for your arrival. She has a large dresser filled with onesies and pants and tops folded meticulously, Marie Kondo-style, and labeled by size. Back in 1990, she was planning the critical moment when the little girls would be piling into the car and concerning herself with the best way to make it work. She knows what people are saying, thinking, implying. She reads a room.

I used to say that when your mom was at Cleveland Heights High School, along with two thousand and more students, she not only knew all their names, but she could tell you what they were wearing on any given day. Only a slight exaggeration. She remains attuned to her many, many good friends. Her social antennae are in good working order.

Watch out, you guys. She will read you like a book.

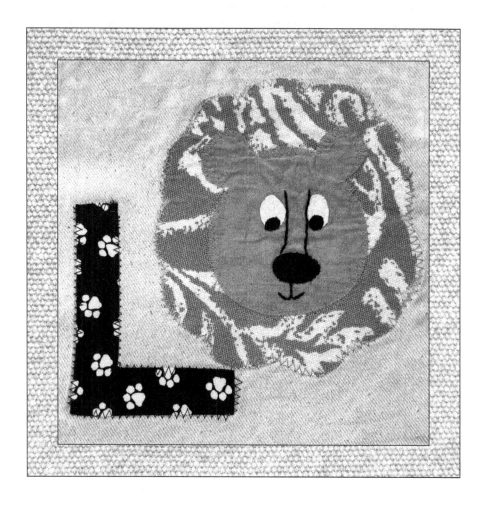

L Is for Lion

As Grandpa and I reach our seventies, we do old-person things that seem normal to us but mark us as elderly to younger people. A few years ago, some young men were moving our furniture in order to refinish the hardwood floors. As they carried a bookcase out of the living room, one said to the other, "See those books with the red covers? Those are old-time maps people used to use." To us, these are present-day maps of Cuyahoga and surrounding counties. Even with GPS on our phones, we occasionally refer to old-time maps.

In our bedroom, our first extension phone still sits on the bedside table next to where I sleep. Not only is it a landline phone with a rotary dial; it's a Snoopy phone, purchased, like a lot of Peanuts stuff, for Grandpa by his mom, your mom's grandmother. It's a foot-tall black and white plastic Snoopy on a red base. Snoopy holds a yellow receiver in his right paw. It never occurs to us to get rid of it.

Grandpa always loved the Peanuts comic strip. He wrote a letter to its creator, Charles Schulz, suggesting a new character, Pigpen's cousin, and Schulz sent back a pencil sketch of the character, "Pigpen's cousin John Ewing," which adorns our living-room wall. In his childhood, Grandpa went so far as to form a Peanuts Club, headquartered in a storage room in the basement of their house. The Peanuts Club hosted an annual carnival and published a neighborhood newspaper, the *Peanuts Press*. Their main activity, as for most kids' clubs, seemed to be making rules. One statute forbade Ghoulardi talk, such as "Hey, group!" and "Turn blue!" (Ghoulardi hosted a popular horror movie show on a Cleveland TV station in the 1960s.) Members included Grandpa's best friend, Joel Couch, and Grandpa's sister, your great-aunt Barbara. I believe the homemade Peanuts Club sign still hangs in the Canton house where Aunt Barb now lives. Grandma Ewing scooped up Peanuts paraphernalia for him far into his adulthood, often at craft shows she frequented. We still have Snoopy books, Christmas decorations, wall hangings, bobble-heads, and games. Still. Still have them.

Next to the venerable Peanuts phone on the bedside table sits a digital clock radio, which I assume is also "old-time." I rely on the alarm clock and play the radio when I'm sewing in our bedroom, whereas younger folks rely on their phones both to wake them up and to entertain them. Our bedroom's sewing accoutrements could shift into your mom's old bedroom, where I now store most of my clothes. Theoretically that is also my yoga room, *theoretically* being the operative word. But moving everything would be a chore, and our bedroom is the warmest room in the house. Its heat is serving me well during this chilly pandemic winter of sewing.

Radio reception is iffy. I can't always tune in to the NPR station I like, whereupon I listen to an oldies station called 106.5 The Lake. "We play anything," they proclaim, which does not seem like much of an endorsement to me. In fact, they do not actually play "anything," such as Patti Paige or Glenn Miller or even Elvis Presley. Instead, their playlist is mainly from the seventies and eighties. While I sew, I hear mostly very familiar songs I'm not crazy about. When I share with your grandfather my theory that oldies stations play "Hotel California" approximately every ten minutes, he gives me a familiar look that says, "You exaggerate." Indeed, after I report my theory, weeks pass before I hear "Hotel California" again. But in the meantime, I repeatedly hear "Uptown Girl," "Horse with No Name," and "Ricky, Don't Lose That Number," all of which now run on a continuous loop in my head. Almost every day that I'm sewing I hear Huey Lewis and the News's "Heart of Rock and Roll," very popular in Cleveland, of course, where the heart of rock and roll is still beatin'.

During the late summer and fall, unpleasant campaign ads interrupt the music. One promotes Jerry Cirino, running for Ohio State Senate against Democrat Betsey Rader in Portage and Geauga counties, east of where we live. It employs a not-so-clever play on her last name, calling her Betsey Betrayed-Her. Apparently, Ms. Rader used to work as a corporate attorney and some years ago defended the company against sexual harassment claims. That nasty ad plays about as often as the song I've heard more than any other, Toto's 1982 "Africa."

As the song even now replays (and replays and replays) in my head, many of the lyrics are indistinguishable. I understand that "It's waiting there for you" and "It's gonna take a lot to drag me away from you," and something about what a hundred men or more could never do, but about much of the rest I am uncertain. Reading the lyrics online just now, I remain uncertain. I have no idea what it's about. Kate Miltner, an Internet researcher, tactfully comments in Rolling Stone, "It's more about evoking a feeling than constructing a cohesive narrative." She explains helpfully, "The song appears to be about a guy who has some feelings for a girl, and then there's some mythological references."

It's the Internet's favorite song, according to Jessica Furseth, writing for *Vice*. It's consoling, nostalgic, melodic, evocative, and transporting. It's also ubiquitous. *Rolling Stone*'s Rob Sheffield writes, "This damn song follows you everywhere, like the sound of wild dogs crying out in the night."

It's not necessarily about Africa, though. *Rolling Stone* points out that CBS haplessly played the song for Nelson Mandela's funeral. Even Toto tweeted that this was inappropriate because its connection to Africa is tenuous at best. To clarify another lyric that you can easily decipher, Kilimanjaro does not arise from the Serengeti. It is not even visible from the Serengeti. And the reference to the Greek mountain Olympus is, at best, cryptic.

Coincidentally, Grandpa and I recently read Ernest Hemingway's famous short story, "The Snows of Kilimanjaro," also connected in a roundabout way to the omnipresent election news. On a PBS talk show recently, a speechwriter for Senator John McCain named Mark Salter choked up talking about it. He recalled how McCain read this story about death aloud to staff and family shortly before his death. I had read "Kilimanjaro" many times but was happy to read it again to keep Grandpa company.

I am hoping to connect all these matters to the lion on the L page, but, unfortunately, lions do not appear in Toto's "Africa," nor even in Hemingway's story, though you can still find at least one unfortunate photograph of Hemingway online posing with his real-life lion kill. His story does include a famous epigraph about a leopard carcass on the side of the mountain. I could have made L stand for leopard, but I had no idea what direction this writing would take. Who knew I'd be hearing Toto's "Africa" on the radio and reading "The Snows of Kilimanjaro"? Also I would have had to design a leopard appliqué myself instead of using the pattern.

The pattern provides a cute lion, and its fusing and stitching cause no problems. Even the curves of the lion and its mane are pretty easy, so I don't know why the bear caused me such fits. The bear's turns are tighter, I guess. I am gratified to use my pawprint fabric once again. It makes for a tidy upstanding L

The letter L started as *el*, a cane shape that meant "god" to the Phoenicians. The Semites reversed the letter and called it *lamed*, meaning "cattle prod." The Greeks flipped the letter in the direction we're familiar with and called it *lambda* (λ). This has given rise to a word describing a speech problem I had never heard of before: lambdacism, an excessive use of the L sound, as when a little kid pronounces her Rs like Ls. Related problems are rhotacism (problems pronouncing R) and sigmatism (problems with S, or a lisp). I had no acquaintance with these fancy words before this investigation into the alphabet.

In a book about babies and grandmothers, the letter L must also stand for love.

You've been in my dreams recently, or at least somebody's babies have been. The outlines are hazy, just like you, but there were definitely babies, and I think in one dream your dad was holding one of you. I've also dreamed that you were triplets instead of twins. Instead of holding up two fingers when I tell people about you, in my dream I held up three fingers. When I described this dream to your mom, she said, "Shut up."

I believe my dreaming is connected with another twin birth I know about. An old friend named Sarah, a little older than your mom, a girl we went to church with, gave birth to twin boys recently. She posted pictures, and the one that struck me showed her husband with both of their new babies. I'm a sucker for dads, dads who care tenderly for their babies and children. One baby lay balanced on his arm and the other rested beside him on the couch, two little bundles like you will be in a few months.

Your dad is very excited about you, and I look forward to seeing him holding you and caring for you.

Sarah posted about her new reality. "Chris and I are abundantly grateful for these lil' humans whom we are already madly in love with. Also we are extremely thankful for our community who have shown up strong in support of our new family of four," she wrote. And I was struck by how life changes, as everyone always warns you, when children come. Your mom and dad's lives will change forever. It's not merely losing sleep and reorienting your schedule and your meals and your household to new members. It's all that, of course. But what I didn't realize before I had kids, and not even until they started to grow up, is something that our friend Fran recently emailed me: that you recover from childbirth but you never recover from parenthood. I still worry about your mom and Uncle Doug. My friends and I, even now, spend an inordinate amount of time talking about our kids, how much we miss them, and what we love about them and, sometimes, what we would change about them if we could.

Your mom and dad are embarking on an adventure that lasts for life. As long as they live, they'll be devoted to you and love you and want the best for you.

Don't be offended if this makes me a little bit sad. We're all so happy about you, and our lives will be richer for knowing you. You'll make us laugh. But one of my favorite phrases in literature is the Roman poet Vergil's *lacrimae rerum*, meaning, "the tears of things." The whole experience of parenthood has tears in it.

My little girl grew up and moved away, and now she's growing up a little more, by one more step. It makes me deeply happy and a little bit sad at the same time. In his poem "Daisy," Francis Thompson (deftly using chiasmus; see X) expressed the paradox in one line: "All the sadness in the sweet/the sweetness in the sad."

M Is for Moon

SOMETIMES YOU MAKE A MISTAKE BY FOLLOWING directions. I know. That's not what I said earlier. I told you to follow directions. Even so, the pattern directions for "M Is for Moon" led me astray.

Counter-intuitively, this is the first page I completed. After I cut out all the letters in alphabetical order, they are fused to and sewn on the pages beginning in the middle of the alphabet. The double page in the middle of the book has M on the left side and N on the right. Even though it is the first one completed, this page's ultimate look turns out to be one of my favorites. I like the yellow fabric of the moon and the dark blue fabric of the M, which includes a smiling moon in its design! My zigzag stitching around them is practically perfect. The crescent moon's little face looks just right.

Before I go on, here's a little moon digression. A gorgeous full moon appeared for Halloween last night. It was a blue moon. A blue moon is the second full moon in a month, a rare occurrence, hence the expression "once in a blue moon." They're usually not blue. A literal blue moon occurs when a certain particulate in the atmosphere alters its perceived color. For example, after a volcanic eruption, the moon may appear blue from our earthly perspective. Because that's also rare, the two ideas merged, and each is referred to as a "blue moon." Ours last night was unusually close to Mars, which made for spectacular brightness. Your book's moon, of course, is merely a fraction of a full moon. We call it a crescent.

You might guess that this usage is related to the French croissant, which has a half-moon shape, and you'd be right. But the Latin root *crescere* doesn't refer to a shape. It means "to grow." Musicians understand the

Italian instruction *crescendo*, meaning to increase volume, often followed by a *decrescendo*. The crescent moon, then, is in the process of increasing. And that moon shape came to be equated with the shape itself. Another derivative, *crew*, is a group of reinforcements, an increase in forces.

The letter itself comes from the Greek letter *mu*, which ultimately derives from a pictograph signifying waves of water. The Egyptian hieroglyph was a series of five peaks, like ripples. The Semites reduced the peaks to three and named the letter *mem*, which means "water." The Greeks cut the ripples down to two.

Now back to your sweet little M page and your book's troublesome directions, which call for "tear away stabilizer" to be stitched behind each appliqué on every page of the alphabet book. That is, the letters and images are cut out with adhesive ironed on to the back. Then they are pressed onto the book pages and stitched all around. The stabilizer is an additional layer that I have never used before. I assume, based on its name, it provides a little stability for the page, so that, as you stitch all around the appliqués, the fabric doesn't pucker or pull. I dutifully pin the stabilizer to the back of the fabric and do an exquisite job, if I do say so, of stitching the M and the moon along with the stabilizer.

I immediately make some halfhearted attempts to remove the stabilizer from the back of the M page, which, as its name implies, is supposed to tear away. Large chucks of it rip off easily, but shreds remain stuck near the stitches and threaten to pull them out. I begin picking away at the stitches, trying pointy items like shears and a knitting needle to tug away the paper. Mostly I procrastinate because I realize it's going to be a tedious slog to tear away all the paper backing. I have the sense to eschew stabilizer—better described as "non-tear-away"—for the remaining pages.

Finally, after I've finished most of the pages, I set to work removing all the stabilizer from the M page. I google "removing tear-away stabilizer" and am both gratified and chagrined to find that many before me have found this task problematic. Helpful seamstresses suggest tweezers and rippers. I spend over an hour hunched over the fabric tweezing and ripping out bits of paper. I eventually bring the page downstairs while your grandfather and I watch *Nationtime*, a restored documentary about the 1972 National Black Political Convention, in which speakers like Richard Hatcher, mayor of Gary, Indiana, and Jesse Jackson (whom I once voted for in a Democratic primary) espouse a notion of racial equality that sounds like what people are saying now in street demonstrations protesting police violence. It is a movie as much for listening as for watching and allows for tugging on minute shreds of paper.

Unfortunately, many stitches come out along with the bits of paper. So much for my perfect stitching. I resew over the parts that have been pulled out. You can see where these filled-in parts are. I could remove all the stitches and start from scratch, but I fear making a mess of the whole thing. Back upstairs I sweep up the tiny shreds of paper stabilizer all over the floor. The usual dust bunnies lie all around. Tons of pins and fabric shreds. I dust and sweep and fold all the fabric remnants. I put all the sewing notions away. Much better. I thank Grandpa for never complaining about all the mess and clutter that makes it difficult for him to reach his dresser. He says he hasn't noticed.

We have to mention masks on this M page, not only because I've been making them but because everybody's wearing them. When the pandemic began, wearing masks seemed bizarre, so weird. Chinese people on the news were wearing masks early on, but they weren't recommended here because healthcare workers needed them first and they were hard to get. Also, Dr. Anthony Fauci, director of the National Institute of Allergy and Infectious Diseases, worried that we might touch our faces more if we were wearing masks. Now, at least where we live, everyone wears masks in public. So unimaginable a few months ago, it's entirely normal now.

M, for me in this strange isolated time at home, might also stand for minimalism. We're extremely lucky that last Thanksgiving, 2019, your parents engineered the replacement of our tiny old TV set with a 55-inch state-of-the-art miracle machine. (See T.) What would your grandfather have done over all these months of banishment from the Cleveland Cinematheque and in-person movies? He watches a film virtually every night, and we now have easy access to Amazon Prime, Netflix, and YouTube. When Grandpa isn't around, I explore YouTube and have been watching videos about minimalism, a fashionable trend to declutter drastically. (I know, it's ironic to be exploring minimalism on a brand-new, giant TV.) This will be an even bigger joke to you if you remember our house as you read this, assuming my current decluttering efforts are limited. Packed full. Chock full. Not quite hoarders, but almost, and Uncle Doug we better not talk about.

Motivated by the minimalism videos I've been watching, I run around the house on the rare day when Grandpa has gone to the Institute of Art. I gather up "gifts" from a crate I've stored for years in our office for emergencies. As any of the preternaturally calm young women on YouTube could have told me, guess what? The gifts year after year have not been given. Nicholas Kristof and Sheryl WuDunn's awesome *Half the Sky*, for example, includes inspiring stories about the condition of women around the world, but a lot of it is so horrific you hate to sadden someone's birthday or Christmas with it. I have copies of some historical fiction that I never really liked, so with whom would I want to share it? And the decorative bottles I was going to fill with homemade vanilla or caramel? Look! I didn't do it! I planned to regift a canvas wine carrier, but we hardly drink wine, almost never carry it anywhere, and rarely give wine as a gift.

All this stuff and more I pack up and tote to my car, along with a bunch of other bags that have been accumulating on the attic steps to give away. A makeup mirror from the 1970s. A bent shoe rack. Some of Grandpa's old shirts. I run out to the car so nobody will come home in time to ask me any questions. Decluttering is not for sissies.

A calming tip is to listen to music as you're decluttering. Grandpa gave me ear buds for Christmas, which allow me to listen to the iPod your mom gave me some years ago as I clean up. Making it an exponentially more meaningful gift, she programmed it for me, with Beatles and James Taylor songs I love, but also her own selections by Alanis Morissette and other artists I never heard of.

Music makes me aware of how close to the surface my emotions are. I tear up listening to a song that reminds me of your mom or to a song I don't even like especially, like Bruce Springsteen's "Secret Garden" from *Jerry Maguire*, which makes my eyes water, and I don't know why. I just tear up. On this pandemic phenomenon, a physician quoted in the *Sydney Morning Herald* says, "[T]his tearing up at any given moment—by people from all walks of life—is the new normal."

Music is not the only stimulus. Today in the car I heard that former Secretary of State George Shultz died at the age of 100. That's not why I cried. His working for Ronald Reagan made me not so much of a fan. Then they introduced Madeleine Albright to comment. I'm not even such a fan of hers, though she served a Democrat, President Bill Clinton.

When *The World*'s Marco Werman welcomed her to reflect on the life of George Schultz, this Democrat immediately responded, "It's my honor that you asked me." Things are so bad, our politics so poisonous, vaccines and COVID variants so worrisome, that all it takes is a relatively generous human impulse to make tears spring to my eyes. At the end of the interview, Albright said that Shultz was a philosopher, a dreamer, and a scientist, which she called "the best combination of characteristics for anyone to have," and I realized tearfully that I had never appreciated George Shultz.

This kind of unpredictable crying seems unique to this pandemic time. I feel just fine, and then a song will happen, or I'll read some words, or a story will come on the news—not even pandemic-related—and suddenly my eyes will sting and my chest will heave a few times. I don't actually break down weeping. The feeling goes away. For just a moment, the emotion and anxiety and grief, the abnormality right under the surface, erupt. It happens over and over.

N Is for Nest

AT THE BACK OF OUR CLEVELAND HEIGHTS HOUSE IS A second-floor porch that looks out on an overgrown apple tree in the backyard. Visitors have commented that the porch feels like a tree house. I make the most use of the porch, Doug is maybe second. Over the years I've gone to the porch to think or cry, to read or just to enjoy a lovely day or a peaceful rainfall. A few times every summer, we cart plates and silverware and bowls of food upstairs for supper on the porch. Doug often celebrates his June 21 birthday there. We have our chocolate cake and watch him open gifts on that longest evening of the year.

At home so much because of the lockdown, I spend many 2020 afternoons sitting on the porch doing needlework or reading. Grandpa and I are hanging out with *Don Quixote*, a nine-hundred-plus-page tome, for the first time, in a translation by Edith Grossman, which I recommend (I who know nothing of other translations or of Spanish, for that matter) because it is readable and the notes informative and not intrusive. This is my second or third run at *Don Quixote*. Previously put off by its epic length and by some of the antiquated language in other translations, this time I push through the long, sometimes repetitious speeches, enjoying the humor and realizing that the story really does move along if you give it a chance.

As it chugs along and I realize how modern the book seems, I pick up another book, called *The Man Who Invented Fiction: How Cervantes Ushered in the Modern World*, by William Egginton, to help reinforce my understanding of the book. What does modern mean as applied to a book written more than four hundred years ago? Cervantes enables us to see the interior lives of his characters, not merely their adventures, as in other romances of his era. The author himself, or at least the narrator, demonstrates a wry self-awareness. In the second half of the book, his characters critique the first half. We moderns usually take credit for such sly self-referencing. *Don Quixote* is modern in that it reflects back on itself. In part, it's a story about stories, a book about books. It's writing about writing. It's like a book about the alphabet, about the letter N from the Greek *nu*, from the Semitic word *nun*, which meant "eel" or "fish."

What does this have to do with N or with nests? you may be wondering. As I sit on the porch hanging out with Don Quixote, counting two hundred pages, three hundred pages, directly in my line of sight whenever I look up from the page, in a cozy fork in the apple tree, is a blue jay nest. It takes a while for me to notice it. We frequently have blue jays in our yard and put peanuts out for them to snack on. I notice that the birds seem to be zeroing in on one spot in the middle of the tree—duh—and suddenly the nest materializes before my eyes. It looks a mess, with a white plastic filament dangling crazily from one side that resembles the plastic string I occasionally replace in our border trimmer. In reading about blue jays, I learn that they frequently incorporate one white material in the outer part of their nest. Our blue jays have apparently read this website. The appliqué nest in your book, I must say, is much neater than a blue jay's. So neat it hardly looks like a nest. It whispers the suggestion of a nest, and the blue ovals allude vaguely to robin's eggs.

I bring binoculars to the porch and learn to focus on the nest. I wait for a parent to alight and then train the lenses on the birds' sheer perfect pattern of blue and black and white. After a week or two of watching the parents take turns sitting on the nest, I hear faint peeping. Eventually I can discern tiny open mouths, three or four, pointing up to the sky as the parents gracefully swoop toward them. After a feeding, the parent bird scooches in, back and forth, right on top of the babies. Every now and then, I worry that a big storm will knock the nest out of the tree or that a squirrel or predatory bird will attack it. I watch for weeks while I read and sew. I tell Doug and Grandpa about the babies, and they come and watch along with me sometimes.

Then a few sultry days pass by, too hot to sit outside. When I return at last to the porch, the nest seems deserted, and there are no blue jays in sight. Either something catastrophic has befallen them, or they have fledged that quickly. If they left the nest, we should have six blue jays flying around our yard, but they seem to have all vanished at once.

A day or two later I am nosing around the flower patch Grandpa planted in the back corner of our yard. Roxie is with me. A lot of squawking erupts from above, and when I look up into the trees, I see a bunch (a flock?) of blue jays hanging out. They don't hold still long enough for me to count them. I figure that the fledged young are practicing flying close to home, learning from their parents, but I'm unable to make out who is who. They all look about the same, but then I decide that a couple appear, well, adolescent. One bird swoops right above my head, clearly wanting me and Roxie out of there, so we beat a retreat. I guess soon after leaving the nest they move into their own neighborhoods because I don't see four or five blue jays at a time anymore. A couple of them still stop by to pick up peanuts. I assume they're the parents, and they're left here in our backyard while their young have moved on to new homes and adventures. It all happens in a matter of months.

I'm writing in November, and today your mom sends us ultrasound pictures of you. Each of you is visible with the profile of a head clearly outlined. When your mom's looking at the screen, she can see you moving around, the girl situated lower, close to the cervix, and the boy higher up. The pictures look like full-sized babies, but you're still tiny, only about five inches long. We don't know your names. But we can see you with our technology; we know you're there, being nourished in your nest by your mom. All four of you are far away from us in Cleveland, though you're in my thoughts all day as I stitch a yellow border around the outside of the nest page.

Your mom flew away to Brooklyn to live and raise her young. She and your dad will teach you to survive, and in twenty years or so, more or less, you'll fly away. As you read this, someday in a vague future, you may have already fledged.

O Is for Octopus

Your Latin teacher grandmother feels compelled to explain that *octo* in Latin means "eight." The "-pus" of *octopus* is related to *pedis*, for "foot." More accurately, though, the word originates in ancient Greek—*okto* plus *pous*. Our book's octopus and a real-life octopus both have eight feet, or more accurately, eight legs. Remember to leave Latin by the wayside when making the word plural. That is, the Latin plural *octopi* is an error, because the word is Greek and not Latin; it's not analogous to the word *cactus*. A fancy plural for this word is *octopodes*, which seems pretentious. Opt instead for the simple Anglicized *octopuses*.

The Egyptians invented the letter O as a hieroglyph meaning "eye," a simple circle like the octopus's eye. The Greeks borrowed it, calling it *omicron*, which literally means "small o"—as in *micro*—and used it for the short O sound. *Omega*, at the end of their alphabet, represented the long O sound. It's the large O—the *mega*. The omicron coronavirus variant, months after the scope of this book, quickly overtook the delta variant. At that point, COVID would have only nine letters remaining to finish the Greek alphabet names.

The resemblance between real octopuses and the one in your book ceases with the number of legs. Real octopuses do not have yellow faces or even recognizable faces, and are not truly green. In fact, they can be almost any color at all because they change color to hide themselves. Their color varies from white to gray to green, yellow, orange, red, brown, and black. They also lack cute expressions. They have eyes, of course, and a mouth that lies under what's called a beak. They're so smushy and protean it's hard to orient yourself to an actual shape. In Sy Montgomery's *The Soul of an*

Octopus (part of my COVID reading) she writes, "One online video shows the animal altering its body position, color, and skin texture to morph itself into a flatfish, then several sea snakes, and finally a poisonous lionfish—all in a matter of seconds." In so many ways, they're alien creatures. Their eight appendages possess dozens of suckers by which they not only grasp surfaces and prey, but taste! Montgomery quotes an octopus researcher as saying, "There's nothing as peculiar as an octopus."

I feel very knowledgeable right now because, in addition to reading Montgomery's book, I just finished watching a popular Netflix documentary called *My Octopus Teacher*. The filmmaker, Craig Foster, made friends with an octopus in an ocean kelp forest off the coast of South Africa where Foster regularly dived. The film follows the course of their relationship as well as the course (spoiler alert!) of the octopus's life over about one year, but the movie took ten years to complete. It shows the eerie undersea world of sharks and crabs and lobsters and obscure translucent otherworldly creatures. It includes a truly heart-stopping pursuit of the octopus by a shark. It's like a chase scene in an action movie, with the octopus (sorry again for the spoiler) literally outwitting the shark.

As most people know, octopuses are remarkably intelligent. They're not at all social. Parents don't stick around to care for their young, like our backyard blue jays, so everything they know they must learn on their own, including strategies for hunting and avoiding predators. Asocial as they are, their intelligence makes them curious, and that's how Craig and the movie's octopus become friendly. The inquisitive octopus eventually reaches out an arm to touch him. It's a very moving moment. You can still find this Oscar-winning movie somewhere, I'm sure. I recommend that you watch it as soon as you're old enough.

Craig was feeling disconnected and depressed before he started diving, but the octopus taught him that he isn't alone and that he is a part of nature. We belong here. You belong here. You belong to our family, through me out here in the world and you in utero. Me staring at my phone for hours every day seeking good news and you swimming around in your natural habitat like the octopus. In my world, right now, the president is contesting the election, and his supporters have been promoting and threatening violence, and it at last occurs. In May 2020, a man named George Floyd was murdered by a policeman as a teenage girl recorded his horrific death on her telephone. It's all overwhelming, tragic, and horrifying. Plus, I might have mentioned that we're in the middle of a pandemic, which is worsening all the time. Good to hide away under the sea for a while. The octopus has serious problems to contend with, but at least her problems are different from mine.

I need the distraction of creating an "O Is for Octopus" page. I know the cutting and sewing around the legs and even around the O is challenging. I decide to stitch the O by hand, wanting to use my embroidery skills, such as they are, in a couple of places, as with the bear. The stitches have to lie close together, and pushing a needle through the stiff appliqué is arduous, making the whole task challenging. The stitching comes out looking not meticulous, but adequate. The green fabrics are from the remnants I bought for making Christmas masks.

The pattern's instructions recommend overlapping the images over the letter. In fact, overlapping is necessary because the pages aren't big enough for both the letter appliqué and the image. The octopus's many legs hog the whole page. I put the letter over part of the octopus, because if you're learning the alphabet from this book you should be able to see the whole letter. I don't make that choice on every page, but the obtrusive octopus would cover almost half of the O. Covering up letters doesn't seem an effective way to teach you the alphabet.

Obtrusive octopus reminds me of a family activity we call Stephanie's Game, after your cousin Stephanie. She introduced us to it one Christmas Eve when we were all celebrating the holiday at our house. A version of this game, Scattergories, is sold at stores, but there's no need to buy it. Each person suggests one category, such as makes of car or breakfast foods. All the players write these categories across the top of a paper to make a graph. Along the left side of the paper, each player calls out a letter of the alphabet. Our little alphabet book has provided you with raw materials to choose from. In an agreed-upon amount of time, say ten minutes, everyone tries to think of an item in the category that starts with the required letters. So for C, R, and T, your car companies could be Chevrolet, Rolls Royce, and Tesla. Rolls Royce would earn you extra points for using the beginning letter twice. If someone else thinks of it as well, neither of you earns any points.

If someday you're playing Stephanie's game, and the category happens to be, say bold animals, and one of your letters is O, you could write obtrusive octopus and score double points. Keep that in mind if you ever play the game.

P Is for Penguin

THE ANCESTOR OF P WAS CALLED *PE*, THE SEMITIC WORD for *mouth*, and it was shaped like a mouth. Over many centuries, the Phoenicians changed its shape to look like a hooked sickle, the Greeks squared the hook to make what we recognize as *pi* (Π), and the Romans transformed it into what we recognize as a P. A linguist describes its sound as the voiceless bilabial plosive, that is, the sound you make at the beginning of *penguin*.

Only a few things come to mind about penguins. Your Great Aunt Betty (my dad's sister) and her husband, Rudy, were bird watchers who did a lot of traveling. They even traveled to Antarctica and brought back 16 mm footage of penguins. I would have been in high school then. When they visited our home in Canton, they would set up the projector and a screen in our living room and show us their fancy home movies and narrate them. It was quite a show. Betty would interrupt Rudy's narration to correct him about something, and he'd contradict her, and that would go on for a while as the reels unspooled. For a brief time back then, I knew a bunch about different varieties of penguins and where they live. If you ever have a chance, watch the old documentary *March of the Penguins*, a wonderful film.

My only other penguin connection is through my friend Mara, who has four boys, the youngest of whom is, at the time I'm writing, obsessed with penguins. She posted on Facebook about how one day Gus, who's seven, asked if he could climb into her lap. Once there, he mused about growing up, which he estimated would take about eleven more years. He didn't intend to marry, but would instead move in with a roommate and hoped his mom would continue to do his laundry. He'd come over about once a week for dinner. For a career, he was considering running a pizza shop called Penguin's Pizza. His parents would enjoy free delivery. Mara commented that every time he asks to sit on her lap, she will say yes. He can come over for dinner anytime he wants to, she added, but she draws the line on doing his laundry. As I write, Gus has fifteen stuffed toy penguins (he's going to leave a few at home for Mara when he grows up), writes stories about penguins, talks about penguins, watches videos of penguins, and visits them at the Cleveland Metroparks Zoo.

Which I hope you also will do.

Cleveland's penguins are black footed and are native to South Africa. They have neither orange feet nor orange beaks like the penguin in your book. There are about twenty-eight varieties of penguins, but their common name comes from the Latin word *pinguinus*, which means "plump." Our fancy English word *pinguid* means "fat" or "oily." Some scholars, however, believe that penguin comes from the Welsh words for "white head." Their family name is *Spheniscidae*, from the Greek word for "wedge shaped," which describes their wings. The Germanic word is *fett gans*, or fat goose. Penguins aren't really fat, of course. They just have expansive waistlines. Fossils of giant penguins found off New Zealand and Antarctica are as tall as a man, almost six feet. Some varieties, the megadyptes (great divers) and the eudyptes (good divers), do have orangish beaks and feet, but not as brilliant an orange as is in your book.

A search for that orange fabric compels me into our attic where I vaguely remember there being some orange fabric long ago. When your Uncle Doug was in kindergarten, we would walk the several blocks along with some neighborhood kids and moms up to Noble School, where an orange-vested crossing guard held up a sign to stop traffic and allow us to cross. Doug was fascinated by that guy.

On Halloween he wanted to dress as a crossing guard. I bought the bright orange fabric and stitched a primitive vest. We had a plastic police badge and put that on it and had some kind of headgear as well. Your grandfather prides himself on creative and interesting costumes, and he always looked askance at this one, but he wasn't going to make or sew one, was he? And Doug was happy and looked cute.

Along with that orange remnant, I find a yard or two of heavy black denim. That was for your mom's witch costume one year, and it served as a cape, if not a black dress. That has come in handy, not least for the penguin himself.

If you look closely at the penguin's white belly, you'll see little snowflakes on the fabric that helped make those Christmas COVID masks. I like how the snowflakes work for the penguin. They're not so appropriate for the dog's, cat's, and whale's eyes, but for the penguin, they're perfect.

I hand-stitch around the beak and feet, as I did for the octopus. Mostly,

I find the machine's zigzag stitching works pretty well, but every now and then I pull out the old needle and embroidery thread.

Pandemic, a P word with some currency, would have been difficult to represent with an appliqué. For almost everyone other than Gus, it's the P word of the moment. As I write, the US death toll is 352,000, but it will be many more by the time I finish writing this book. Yesterday President Trump tweeted that the Centers for Disease Control had exaggerated this number. A friend's husband suggests on Facebook that official statistics on COVID deaths are "cooked up." These conspiracy theories never explain the motive for these purported lies, just vague allusions to liberals trying to control everyone. I imagine they don't know any real doctors and nurses, who I can't imagine are faking their worry, fear, and grief.

I've been lucky. Most of my friends and acquaintances who have contracted it have recovered. At least two of them are suffering from long COVID, however. Their symptoms include extreme fatigue, aches, and brain fog. My old church friend, Sam, died of COVID, as did a friend's husband. So far, that's my experience.

The disease was declared a pandemic by the World Health Organization on March 11, 2020, a week after my last class at Cleveland State before spring break. It's really a pan-epidemic, a disease spreading to people everywhere. *Pan* means "everywhere." The *-dem* syllable means "people," as in democracy and demography. COVID was already an epidemic—*epi-* meaning "upon"—in China. A pandemic is an epidemic that spreads worldwide.

A doctor friend seemed to be recovering from the disease a few weeks after he was diagnosed. Months later he is still battling symptoms of fatigue, pain, and brain fog. He doesn't know how he contracted it. As for us, I monitor every cough, every headache, every ache. I wear my mask and wash my hands, hoping not to catch or to spread the coronavirus. I want to put the lie to the prefix *pan-*, and help bring on a new prefix, *post-*.

Q Is for Quilt

SOURCES SAY THAT Q'S PHOENICIAN ANCESTOR *QUOPH* could have meant monkey or a ball of wool. A monkey would have looked cute in our book. Ball of wool, not so much. As it is, the quilt serves nicely. The Greeks ignored Q. *Kappa* served quite nicely for the same sound.

I've never quilted except for making a small doll's quilt many years ago. Never seriously, and never by hand. Never with quilt batting, which the instructions wanted me to use under the appliqué on the front of the book (which I didn't). Batting is a thin soft layer, like pillow stuffing, that makes quilts thick and warm. This page has a little quilt, minus the batting, which was fun to put together.

I'm not sure the page as a whole works very well, because of how the quilt is arranged on the page. The pattern calls for a five-inch square quilt as well as the letter Q on a page that's only nine by six inches. As I've mentioned, the instructions are always suggesting overlapping the letter with part of the image; a five-inch quilt would cover the Q almost entirely. Instead, I fold the quilt over so that most of the letter Q shows. The fold forms a little pocket, for which I fashion twin dolls to tuck inside.

On every page, you and your future are in my mind. I picture your mom and dad or even me reading the book with you and pulling out those little figures to look at. I realize that tiny dolls will have to be removed for quite some time, lest you babies stick them in your mouths. No doubt they'll quickly be lost in the wash or whatever. Hence, I have not devoted a ton of time to creating them, but even so, designing and cutting them neatly challenge my meager skills.

I considered making a little boy doll and a little girl doll because I have learned your genders by the time I reach this page. But that would require what? Cutting out different hairstyles? Putting the girl in a little skirt and the boy in little pants? That's so twentieth century! Besides taxing my minimal competence. I choose to fashion identical dolls made with different fabrics to coordinate with the quilt. As with other pages, the most fun part is picking out the fabrics for everything, and because the quilt uses three different ones, extra fun!

The letter Q is (as I'm sure you've noticed) the same fabric as the giraffe and the lion and the dog's face and ears. I bought a lot of this fabric many years ago to use for a tote bag pattern. I used it instead for some placemats and napkins but still have reams of it left. That's why you see it scattered here and there throughout the book.

Grandma Ewing, your grandpa's mom, quilted for a while along with Aunt Penni, your great aunt. It's a popular hobby now, and back in the 1980s it also enjoyed a vogue. Though the two of them took some classes at a nearby Canton store, I don't think they ever completed a quilt, maybe just small quilting projects. It's hard even thinking of Grandma Ewing doing this because as long as I knew her, from the mid-1970s on, her eyesight was damaged from diabetes.

I recall her sitting on a stool at a counter under a bright fluorescent light in her kitchen, holding a magnifying glass over Land's End and L.L.Bean catalogs, searching for gifts to buy for all of us. When I married Grandpa, I had never heard of these catalogs. They were a tad too costly for my family. Soon I was wearing these brands. Sometimes before my birthday, Grandma E. would hand me a L.L.Bean catalogue and tell me to mark the things I wanted. I would mark five or ten things, thinking she'd have plenty to choose from. I soon learned that instead she'd buy me everything I marked. She loved to shop, she loved to buy, and she loved giving gifts.

She (I'll call her Dee) had a similar experience with her own mother-in-law, Grandpa's grandma, your great-great-grandmother. The Ewing family owned a successful hardware business, which morphed into a car dealership, Ewing Chevrolet. Dee had come from a modest background; her dad worked for the railroad. Great-great-grandma Ewing used to take Dee and one or more of the grandkids to New York City to shop and see a show. One time, she gave Dee $100 to spend on herself, however she liked. Dee told me how thrilling that was, to be able to spend $100 on whatever she wanted. In later years, when she purchased gifts for me and the rest of the family, she wanted us to feel as she had felt. I felt chagrined, embarrassed, overwhelmed, but also thrilled, loved, and noticed.

My sewing is a byproduct of the current quarantine, a pandemic Q word. We're at home. It's hard to convey how suddenly and shockingly this came upon us. On March 4, 2020, I taught my last regular Latin 101 class at Cleveland State University. That week, I had shared the Latin etymology of coronavirus and the Greek origin of pandemic and explained that the new word COVID stood for "coronavirus disease 2019." I even joked that the students "may have heard something about" the virus because its progress in China and its discovery on our shores were already all over the news. Anyway, I taught fourth conjugation verbs to my eleven students, cheerfully said goodbye, and went home to enjoy our spring break. My office calendar remained turned to March 2020 for two more years.

In the midst of that spring break, the administration decided on an extra week off while they decided how to manage our return. As those days passed and the number of COVID cases rose, it became clear that we wouldn't physically be returning to school in the near future. Instead, we'd teach our classes remotely, using Zoom technology. Even so, we assumed that after a month or so, sometime before the end of the school year, we'd return.

In the meantime, Grandpa's film program at the Cleveland Institute of Art Cinematheque shut down. The man lives and breathes movies, and suddenly, not only his theater but all theaters closed for an indefinite period. He was shocked and angry. The last film at the Cinematheque was *A Hidden Life*, a beautiful, disturbing fictionalized account of Franz Jägerstätter, an Austrian Christian persecuted and executed for resisting the Nazis. I remember chatting in the lobby after the movie, wondering if we should even be there, if it was worth the risk being out in public. But I never thought that it would be way more than a year before I returned to that space. After your birth, as it turned out.

I completed the end of my semester communicating online with my students. Back then, I was intimidated by Zoom technology. I had long taught a version of my class one-on-one; we called it Latin Flex, in which students ploughed through their Latin work mostly on their own, meeting with me once a week. Thinking we could muddle through the end of the semester without meeting even remotely, I offered assignments and help via email and by phone, though no one took advantage of that. I'm sorry now that we didn't use Zoom. I didn't realize it then, but I will never see those students again. Autumn, the bohemian girl with the lip ring who came in late and sat in the back and who I diagnosed as being on the autism spectrum. Will, the diffident guy who missed a class, even before the lockdown, because his uncle had died of COVID. Brittany and Emma, the inseparable stars of the class who grasped every concept the moment it was explained and had to endure my repeating and repeating and repeating. ("An adjective agrees with the noun it modifies in number, gender, and case. Remember?")

When and if I ever return to campus, they'll have to seek me out if we're to meet again. Only a couple of students have stayed in touch. Thrown into a weird regimen of gazing at computer screens, managing messages from professors, and negotiating work schedules during a pandemic (most CSU students work, many of them full time), they must have felt shell-shocked. Many of them kept up with their Latin nonetheless, and I didn't penalize any of them very much if their work slipped drastically.

Like so many others, I'm now Zoom adept. I meet with my sisters, your great-aunts Betsey and Marge every Tuesday; once a week with my friends Marianne and Katie; and regularly with my writing group and book groups.

Last spring and summer, mid-pandemic, I couldn't recruit students for Latin because hardly anyone was on campus. As a result, only nine students signed up for Latin, and the university canceled Latin for the academic year. It was sad, but it was a relief as well. I didn't have to contend with face shields and masks and maintaining a six-foot distance from all my students. And in March, when you two arrive, I won't have to negotiate time off to visit you.

Other people have lost family members and friends. Many of those infected suffer long-term effects. Businesses have closed, and families have been evicted. I'm grateful that my own losses have been slight. Still, sometimes I look back at March 4, 2020, and wonder if that will be my last day ever teaching Latin at CSU.

R Is for Rocket

IN MY LIFE AT THIS MOMENT, IT SEEMS THAT R COULD stand for *ravine*. During this quarantine, Grandpa and I have been taking daily walks, and Grandpa, who usually chooses the location, gravitates toward ravines. He studies a map first—one of our old-fashioned paper ones with a red cover—and zeroes in on a probable ravine. When we arrive, he finds a bridge, overlook, or empty lot from which to gaze down at the ravine. He comments on whether there's water at the bottom. If it's safe to climb down close to the water, we do. He picks up rocks hoping to find a salamander or a crayfish. That's the drill.

Today I finally ask whence this fascination with ravines. The Grand Canyon must have been the ultimate ravine experience, right? "It was, actually," he says. I know I am triggering a familiar story. The Grand Canyon is part of the Western Trip, as he formally calls it, the vacation his family took in 1962 when he was eleven years old. His dad, Stan, your great-grandfather, who was singularly unadventurous and hated being lost, dared to drive the four kids and wife, Dee, who sometimes helped with the driving, out west from Ohio. Uncle David, Grandpa's oldest brother, shared in the driving as well. Stories of this trip frequently arise. Peering over the scary edge of a ravine or any high place, Uncle David and Uncle Jim would grab Grandpa's shoulders roughly, push him forward without letting go, and say, "Saved your life!" Shocking that he's still afraid of heights.

Your grandfather at age eleven was obsessed with national parks and with top-rated AAA motels. He read the AAA guide to help pick out the very best accommodations! They drove in a nine-passenger Chevy station wagon with an extra backward facing seat in the far back.

Arriving at the Grand Canyon after dark, they pulled the wagon up to a cabin near the rim. Everyone piled out of the car, crabby and tired and ready for bed. Grandpa, for some reason, was the first to wake up the next morning. He dressed quietly and stepped outside the cabin. Before him and below him lay the fabulous multi-colored hues, the dizzying depths, the awesome scale of the Grand Canyon. The vastness and its immediacy took him by surprise; ordinarily, they had to drive a while to reach an "attraction." But he saw it all by himself, unexpectedly, early in the morning. "It was a religious experience," he told me.

Other things about that trip were life changing too. Grandpa's new-found love of the American West made him want to see *How the West Was Won* in Cinemascope, the 1962 epic starring Henry Fonda, Gregory Peck, John Wayne, Debbie Reynolds, and many other big stars of the time. Nominated for eight Academy Awards, your grandfather was awestruck when he saw it in New York City in Cinerama. This fondness for such a politically incorrect, imperialist saga would no doubt horrify us even now and, more so, you, in your future wisdom. For a naive, twelve-year-old white boy in 1963, the movie was spectacular. The next step, two years later and back in Ohio, was haranguing Stan and Dee to take him to see the 1953 western *Shane* at a drive-in movie. That sealed the deal. Favorite movie of all time, and a lifelong movie buff was born.

Of course, I was talking only of ravines and the letter R when I brought up the Grand Canyon. Stitching up a ravine appliqué would outstrip my artistic talents. I'm lucky to have only a rocket ship to worry about, and the letter R itself is not too challenging. It derives from the Greek *rho* (P), which looked more like a P. The Romans added the tail and called R the *canina littera*, or dog's letter, because they thought it sounded like a growl.

Rockets are a more significant part of my childhood than they will be of yours, I expect. I was seventeen on July 20, 1969, when Americans first walked on the moon. Newspapers and magazine articles explained how to take a photo of the TV moment when Neil Armstrong's foot touched the moon's surface. I had received a Polaroid camera for my high school graduation. I followed the instructions diligently and preserve the fuzzy black and white photo in an old album. How were we to know that one day and for generations to come, we would be able to watch the entire moon landing via YouTube?

As I think of it, the fuzzy black-and-white image resembles you two in the ultrasound shots your mom sends me.

Today, as I'm writing, is another momentous day for America: November 7, 2020, Joe Biden was declared the winner of the presidential election, with his running mate, Kamala Harris, as vice president. When we went to bed on election night it wasn't clear who the winner was going to be. In the days since, it has become clearer that Biden has won. We waited for several key states—Georgia, Nevada, Arizona, and Pennsylvania—to finish counting the ballots, many of which were mailed in early but counted last. When the news came through this afternoon as news networks decided to announce the inevitability, my phone filled up with messages. My friend Judi was first, saying that her daughter-in-law reported people dancing in the streets in San Francisco. Neighbor Paula told me that there will again be dogs in the White House; the Bidens have two (the Trumps zero). I sent "yay" messages to Aunt Marge and your cousin Stephanie. I wished the book group congratulations. Friends on Facebook were rejoicing. We watched the news much of the afternoon. Tonight we watched Kamala Harris and Joe Biden address the nation.

I teared up a few times, to be sure. The most powerful moment for me came when I watched a video of a favorite pundit, Princeton professor Eddie Glaude, break down with relief on CNN. Two matters, however, mitigated the relief. For one, the vote counting took days, so the delay deprived us of some joyous surprise. Also, Trump's refusal to concede was worrisome. Not that he won't give a formal concession statement—that's too much to hope for. Even his pursuing legal strategies and recounts is not so horrible. What's bad is his insistence that he actually won. He claims that the procedures, especially in Pennsylvania's cities, are corrupt. Telling this to his followers presages the violence in our near future. That takes some of the shine off. At this point, we have no intimation of the insurrection to come.

The true election victory is a balm nonetheless. On a lovely walk through part of Cleveland's Cultural Gardens in shining 60 degree weather, Grandpa and I visit the India installation, with a tall statue of Gandhi looking out over several obelisks describing the strengths of Indian culture. We look over the fence into the ravine, of course, formed by Doan Brook.

We hold hands as we walk.

We stop at Mitchell's Ice Cream by the Cinematheque to celebrate the election. Grandpa enjoys his usual flavor, Coffee Chocolate Chunk. I select a Taster's Duo of Peanut Butter Chocolate Chunk and Salted Caramel. (See? No butter pecan.)

Roxie, another R word, is the star of the day. Numerous people stop to say hi. A woman near the ice cream shop asks whether our Roxie is a shih tzu and describes her little dog named Roxie Ann! Another woman pets Roxie, who seems very glad to meet her, and sadly reports that her black lab Annie had just died this week. She's already yearning for another dog. Roxie seems especially friendly to her, wagging her tail and approaching her repeatedly for a pat on the head. Roxie spreads a little extra happiness today.

Notably also, I sew together the R page, along with the H for Hand, the I for Ice Cream, and the S for Star. With room for a finishing stitch all around, I choose blue.

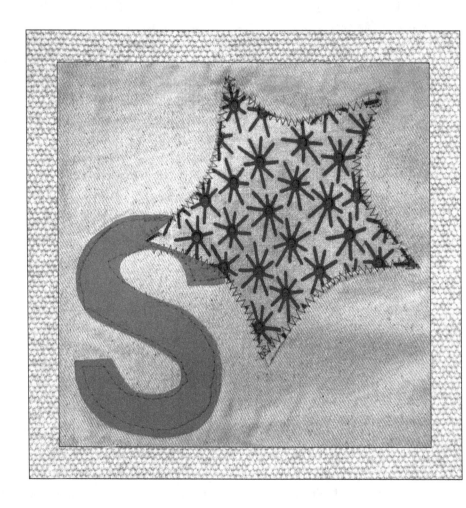

S Is for Star

THE GREEK WORD *SIGMA* (Σ), ANCESTOR OF OUR S, SEEMS
to derive from the Greek word for *hiss*, which makes sense, right? The Semites
and Phoenicians set it horizontally, so it resembled a W, but the Greeks turned
it upright. The Romans smoothed out its angles into the sinuous S we know
today.

Your book's pretty star is easily created. Instead of a predictable gold
or silver fabric, I use old-fashioned flour-sack fabric decorated with red and
blue stars and a coordinating blue for the S. I don't have much to say about
stars, although I like them. Ever since my friend Father Dan Begin died in
2017, a starry sky makes me think of him. He loved learning about astronomy.
Every Epiphany his sermon would describe how Jupiter and Saturn appeared
conjoined in the constellation Pisces in 7 BC and how Jupiter and Venus
danced a similar dance with each other in 3 BC. Either event could have
appeared as the Eastern star that drew the Wise Men to Bethlehem. He
frequently called his congregation's attention to the awesome beauty and size
of the starry sky. Now when I let Roxie out at night before bedtime, I look up.
If the stars are out, I feel like I'm saying hello to Father Dan.

Because I have little expertise with astronomy, though, I'm switching
up the S to stand, first, for *surgery*.

That's how I first met your dad. He's had shoulder surgery himself, but
I met him when your mom needed surgery for thoracic outlet syndrome. In
2014 she was watching a performance of Cirque de Soleil, and when the show
ended, her entire right arm was swollen. The diagnosis took a while, but
eventually doctors figured out she had an extra rib near her collarbone. That
rib was causing vascular difficulties, meaning that the compression near her

shoulder was inhibiting circulation. She'd had that extra rib for twenty-eight years, but suddenly it needed to come out. Her customary diligent research led her to an experienced surgeon in Boston. I flew there to keep her company, and your dad was scoring major boyfriend points, as he put it, by being on hand and providing good company.

While she was in surgery, your dad and I—essentially strangers—spent several hours together. He had already impressed me by reserving a room for me near Massachusetts General Hospital and writing me a nice note before we met, saying that he loved your mom and that he imagined she had inherited some of her lovable qualities from me. He knew how to win over a girlfriend's mother.

We sat for several hours in Mass General's expansive waiting room. During the surgery, volunteers came to find us several times to tell us your mom's operation was going well. In the meantime, your dad told me a lot about his childhood. His dad had been irresponsible, and he no longer had a relationship with him. I heard a lot about it, but I'll leave it to him to share those experiences with you.

S also stands for stories, because that's what I've been thinking about.

This quarantine has provided lots of time for reading, at least for fortunate people like Grandpa and me who can work from home. I am immersed in a series of children's adventure stories, written by Arthur Ransome in the 1930s, the first of which is *Swallows and Amazons*. Perfect escapist COVID reading. Maybe I'll buy you a set sometime.

Also, Marilynne Robinson's *Jack* appeared recently. I read a library copy and feel compelled to reread the second book in this series, *Home*, in which Jack is also a main character. Then I go another step backward to *Gilead*, the first novel in the series, and end with *Lila*, the third book. These melancholy meditations on the meaning and sadness of life concern two families in the fictional small town of Gilead, Iowa. They're stories, and stories within stories, all interlocking the lives of these two families, both with patriarchs who are ministers.

In your mom's childhood we read stories together as part of the bedtime ritual, usually along with Doug. After consuming lots of picture books and Golden Books filled with Sesame Street characters, Donald Duck and his nephews, and the Berenstain Bears, we moved on to chapter books. We revisited *The Wizard of Oz* more than a few times. Motherhood gave me the opportunity to read Laura Ingalls Wilder's *Little House* series for the first time (and second and third). I had the distinct joy of reading aloud my favorite book, *Charlotte's Web*, a bunch of times. I loved sharing *The Chronicles of Narnia* as well as some of my favorites from the Weekly Reader Book Club of my childhood, such as *Mrs. Coverlet's Magicians, Ellie's Problem Dog, Castaways in Lilliput*, and *A Dog on Barkham Street*. We loved *The Secret Garden* and *James and the Giant Peach*. Eventually we made it through *Huckleberry Finn*, with me stumbling over (and trying to explain) the N-word. After Grandma Dee gifted your mom with a couple of American Girl dolls, Samantha and Felicity, we enjoyed the novels that provide the dolls' backstories.

When your mom could read on her own, she adopted those American Girl stories and, in contrast, dearly loved the scary Goosebumps books. Luckily, we lived within walking distance of the Noble Neighborhood Library and visited there frequently, especially as homeschoolers.

Your parents have already accumulated a supply of books for you. They, too, live near a library branch they can walk to. I envy them their nightly reading to you, and you for cuddling and listening to your parents' voices and encountering all these stories—hearing *Goodnight Moon*—for the first time.

I have just finished rereading another children's book, *The Once and Future King*, a 1959 novel by T. H. White. I once considered it one of my favorites but hadn't reread it since the 1960s and retained appallingly little memory about the story. Two things stuck with me: the whimsical humor of the first chapters about King Arthur, called Wart as a boy; and the heartsick melancholy of the final ones, when the kingdom goes to ruin. I'd forgotten nearly all the specifics.

It takes me a few weeks to read my old paperback, 639 pages long, and I am reading other things in between, taking advantage of this blessed (while also dark) expanse of time. I speed through the last several hundred pages, the suspense driving me on. I know the ending isn't happy. That's not exactly a spoiler, because the Sir Thomas Malory gives away the ending in his title, *The Death of Arthur*, which White used as a source.

As I approach the end, I am thinking about stories. I'm writing stories here for you about our family. I hope they make you smile at us. You'll carry with you these stories of families and pets and childhoods, both from this book but even more from your parents and friends and relatives. Then you'll accumulate your own stories to tell. One way to convey them is to use the alphabet you've been given, and collect written words and paragraphs and pages to be carried forward into time.

T. H. White took on the task of rewriting the legend of King Arthur for modern people, full of humor and wit and love. If you read it when you're young, you'll identify with Wart. Later on, you may identify with the tragic love affair of Lancelot and Guenever (as White spells it). That book sat on my shelf for fifty years without being touched. Now those alphabet letters have once again conveyed the story to me, even more poignantly, because I'm in King Arthur's aged shoes as I reread the book in 2021, the year of your birth.

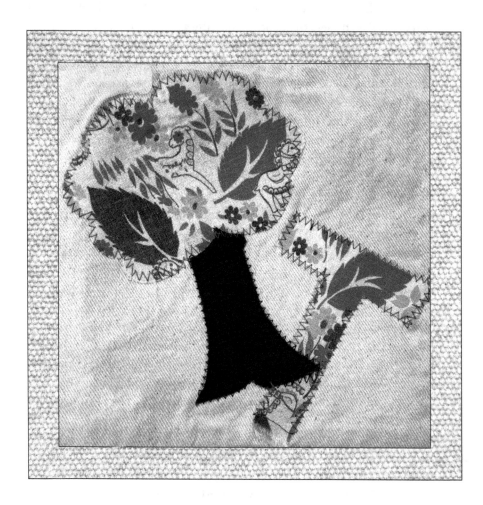

T Is for Tree

OUR LETTER T DERIVES FROM THE SEMITIC *TAU*, WHOSE ancestor may be the Egyptian hieroglyph for a checkmark. The Greeks put the crossbar on the top and also called it *tau* (T), the twentieth letter in their alphabet. It's one of the most common consonants in the English language, appearing in about 7 percent of our words. *The*, after all, is the most common word in English.

My mom's old sacking fabric works out well on this page. The fabric's pattern has trees on it, making it a no-brainer.

Thinking about trees always reminds me of a certain student in a Freshman Comp class at Cleveland State years ago. We may have been discussing a nature essay by a Native American writer, Leslie Marmon Silko or N. Scott Momaday. Anyway, it was something about nature. A young man in my class commented, "I've never especially cared about a tree." He scoffed, looking around the room as though looking for affirmation. "I'm not weird, right?" I think of him almost every time I look admiringly at a tree, which is pretty often. I couldn't, and still can't, figure out how someone, even a handsome callow youth like himself, could never have been dazzled by a tree or fond of a tree. I wonder if he's changed his mind in the meantime.

Your mom and Uncle Doug used to climb the apple tree that was right outside our kitchen window, stretching up to the porch where I sometimes sit sewing or watching the blue jays at their nest. It was our only climbable tree. You could step on the lowest hanging branch and pull yourself up a few more for a pretty good perspective on our yard—not an ambitious goal, but lots of fun when you're a little person. Your mom was always brave, so brave that

I'd hold my breath and try to restrain myself from restraining her. Someone who honeymoons in Thailand—another T—is pretty adventurous. Someone who joins Teach for America at a tough school in New York City is pretty adventurous. Someone who continues to teach at-risk kids in Brooklyn is pretty adventurous. And you two may provide her with the greatest adventure of all.

When I was growing up, our yard also had one tree that was ideal for climbing. There was a willow with a steep trunk that was challenging to clamber up. But on the corner of the front lot stood a maple with a perfect V-shape that you could step up to. Then came a wide, long horizontal branch perfect for sitting on. Your Great-aunt Marge and I used to climb up there and deliberately fall to the ground when a car was passing. We wanted to see if anyone would stop to see if we were okay. The few times a car seemed to be slowing down, we'd jump up and brush ourselves off, terrified they were actually stopping. When Abbie the dog came along, we discovered she was a pretty good tree-climber too.

Grandpa remembers climbing trees with his friends at his next-door neighbor's house. They'd want to see how high they could climb. A little park down the street had a tree house where he and his friends carved their names on the walls. I asked him if the names would still be there, but he didn't know. He says they climbed trees for "a different perspective." I can't leave the subject of tree-climbing without telling you about Joel, Grandpa's best childhood friend, who climbed up the neighbor's evergreen when Doug and your mom lost a toy rocket way up high. He shimmied straight up the trunk. Joel is tall himself. Watching that tall figure climb higher and higher in that massive tree was a sight to behold.

T must also stand for *television* during this weird time at home. Unable to attend concerts, go to restaurants, or visit movie theaters, many of us gather 'round the TV to watch the latest Netflix and HBO offerings. All the talk is of *The Queen's Gambit* (I didn't watch it but liked the book); *The Crown*, with current residents of Buckingham Palace as main characters; and *The Handmaid's Tale*, based on Margaret Atwood's classic novel; and many, many others. Current movies are also available only by streaming on TV because theaters are closed. Movies streaming at home have been a godsend to your grandfather.

First, however, came the godsend of your parents and their determination. When they were last visiting us for Christmas, in 2018, they listened to our jawing about when we were buying a new TV to replace our old, thirteen-inch model, connected only to an aerial, with no access to the riches of Internet and cable. We take a very long time to decide on things. Between themselves, your mom and dad placed a bet on whether we would purchase a new TV by February of 2019. Your mom bet on us, surprisingly, and lost the bet. We did not purchase a new TV.

They visited again almost a year later, the weekend of Thanksgiving, 2019, determined to break our indecisive impasse. I do my fair share of hemming and hawing, but your dad felt the full force of your grandfather's hesitancy to make a decision—because, you know, it might be the wrong decision. Where would we put a new, big screen TV? How would we mount it on a wall? Do we need high definition? How would we have to reconfigure the living room furniture to accommodate it? ("I like the way the living room is configured now!" Grandpa exclaimed at one point.) Every now and then your dad gave me a look, like, really? Does he ever stop asking questions? No, I answered silently. He never stops asking questions.

Eventually, your dad found a deal at Microcenter with the specifications Grandpa required. He explained and explained, over and over, about how we'd likely not find as good a deal, how we should do it now while they were here to help us, and how this model fit all Grandpa's criteria. We drove out to the store, and your dad generously, kindly, sacrificially offered to accompany Grandpa inside the store, while your mom and I peeled off for a scan of craft items at Michaels, where your mom wanted to buy an embroidery kit. "I don't have to live with him," your dad said. "If he's mad at me, it's okay, because I'm leaving in two days."

I loved touring Michaels with your mom. She picked out a little pineapple embroidery hanging and began working on it as soon as we got home.

After our twenty minutes of shopping, your mom and I braved the TV department of Microcenter. As we approached, Grandpa was interrogating a salesperson. Your dad looked at me over their heads and widened his eyes, as if to say, "Wow. The questions keep coming." Grandpa started showing me all the options (everyone's worst nightmare—so many options), while your dad maintained eye contact with me, giving me little shakes of the head for every model. When we reached the last one, your dad gave me a little nod, and I said, "That one looks good. Why don't we just go with that one?" A 55-inch LG OLED smart TV. It had the right number of pixels and everything.

Still, questions persisted, more angst. At some moments it seemed all was lost, but your grandfather finally said okay. We had to wait by the checkout as they fetched our purchase from the warehouse, and I knew the decision could change at any moment. It was like negotiating a complicated bill in Congress. A tenuous agreement can be derailed at any moment.

Sometimes I marvel that he ever marshaled the courage and decisiveness to propose to me. At the time, I had no idea what agonies of indecisiveness he must have suffered.

Grandpa and your dad went out to pull their cars up to the front of the store. The last hurdle after purchasing was fitting the huge box into the car. We slid it into the backseat of your parents' rental, and it became stuck with the back doors open. We pushed, we pulled, we nudged. No luck.

I summoned an employee who was out on the sidewalk after helping another customer. He called over another guy. They pushed, they pulled, they nudged. I kept my eye on your grandpa, thinking he was going to backtrack, that he was going to think this was a bad omen and send the box back inside the store. Your dad stayed calm and good-humored, as did the store employees. Eventually, they jarred it loose. We moved the box from the rental car to the back of Grandpa's.

At home, once again, your dad played a critical role. He set up the TV, answering more questions. He set up apps and programs, connecting us to their Netflix account and patiently teaching us to use the remote.

We did indeed reconfigure the living room. We soon bought a loveseat to place in front of the TV—a rash quick decision by your grandfather! Now we sit side by side to watch *The Office* and *Mr. Bean* reruns after Grandpa's movie of the night has ended and Roxie snuggles in cozily to watch with us.

All this is to say, and Grandpa would concur, that this TV is a boon to us during our COVID adventure. I can't imagine what Grandpa would have done without movies all this time. We couldn't stream them on our little TV, and he wouldn't sin against the cinema gods by watching great films on that lousy little screen. The TV does not equal the movie-going experience or the wonders of 35-millimeter film (to say nothing of 70 mm), but the "picture" (as Grandpa's dad, Stan, used to say) is pretty darn good. Virtually every night, throughout the lockdown, Grandpa has selected a movie to watch. Sometimes it's a Netflix or Amazon Prime offering. Frequently, it's one of the films he's selected to stream through the Cleveland Cinematheque. Occasionally it's a classic on YouTube.

I watch a film of my own choosing now and then: a documentary about Linda Ronstadt and one about Audrey Hepburn, for example. I have a fondness for old *Columbo* shows; I occasionally squeeze one in. I often join Grandpa in his movie choices, but often I don't, because I'm not a fan of Quentin Tarantino and am squeamish about Wong Kar Wai. I don't feel deprived, though. The poor guy has had all his movies snatched away from him, his lifeblood, and he should choose what he wants to watch. So go our evenings.

Then, after the movie, we refresh ourselves with *Schitt's Creek*, another very popular pandemic choice, and when we've finished that, we watch, night after night, the entire run of *The Office*, one of your parents' favorites. Pure pleasure. On my own, I watch the home decorating shows I cited earlier, and enjoy every season of *The Good Place*, a comedy I hope to share with your grandfather eventually.

Books will probably appear discussing what people watched during the pandemic. Because of your parents' determination and stick-to-it-iveness, we joined the culture.

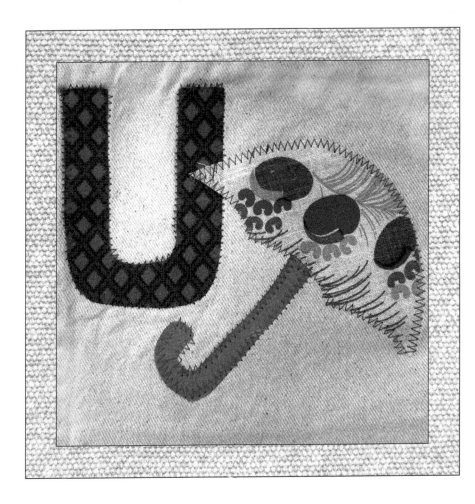

U Is for Umbrella

THE UMBRELLA PROTECTING YOU FROM THE RAIN COMES from *umbra*, the Latin word for "shade" or "shadow," by way of the Italian *ombrella*. During a solar eclipse, the moon forms an umbra, or shadow, on the earth. In a lunar eclipse, the earth forms an umbra on the moon. The earth may also make a penumbra, or "almost shadow," a partial shadow, as it crosses between the sun and the moon. To take umbrage is to be offended or take on a darkened mood, usually because of an insult. The Online Etymology Dictionary compares this usage to the modern slang "throw shade at," meaning "to disrespect" or "criticize." The parasol, in contrast to an umbrella, protects against the sun (*sol*), and if you have unlimited closet space, you might also want to invest in a *paraneige*, which shields you from the snow. The French *neige* derives from *nivis*, the Latin word for "snow."

This has taken us some distance from the letter U, which used to be shaped like a V and was therefore much easier for a Roman stonemason to carve. Beginning in the fourth century, people's handwriting was rounding the bottom. For a time, the U shape signified the vowel sound and the V shape the consonant sound, until they evolved into entirely different letters. That's how W got its name, even though it looks more like double V to us.

On your page, the U is formed from a small square of red print fabric I bought just because I liked it. The umbrella itself comes from some of the old sacking from my mother's house, like the tree for T. I like its old-fashioned look and texture. Because of the red and green in the print, I used some in those Christmas masks I made.

If we had been going out and about in October, we would have needed umbrellas. In 2020 we had forty-five inches of precipitation, twelve more than normal, and many areas suffered from flooding. On October 20 alone, the rainfall for the month doubled. In late November the continuing massive precipitation covered the entire region with a foot of snow. Eighteen to twenty-four inches fell in suburbs farther east, in what we call the Snow Belt, where warm air over Lake Erie sometimes dumps a ton of snow on the region. A *paraneige* is no match for the weather in Chardon or Jefferson, Ohio.

We've always had a lot of snow in northeast Ohio. But based on 100 years of weather data and projections, Ohio temperatures in this newish century—the century in which you'll spend most of your life—might rise by ten or more degrees. This is about the same rise in temperature since the glaciers retreated from Ohio about twelve thousand years ago,

Climate change is one of the most urgent issues in the 2020 presidential election campaign. Donald Trump is of the opinion that it, like so many things, is a hoax. His buddy Tucker Carlson, a host and commentator on Fox News, said recently that "in the hands of Democratic politicians, climate change is like systemic racism in the sky. You can't see it, but rest assured its everywhere and it's deadly." He doesn't believe in either one, in other words, systemic racism or climate change. He once denigrated the affection between Joe and Jill Biden with the comment, "Their love is as real as climate change."

Electing Joe Biden has given us at least a chance. He and his running mate believe it's a real thing. As real as the Bidens' love for each other. As real as systemic racism.

Spring and fall storms, no matter their cause, are no fun for little Roxie, for whom wind, lightning, and thunder are terrifying. The extremes of climate change are not her friend. Your mom used to be afraid of storms too. On Halloween night in 1993, when she was seven, I wrote in my journal that a vigorous wind was keeping her awake. She had been scared by a violent storm in July, and now every storm seemed threatening. I lay down with her for a while, and she asked me why God made bad weather, like wind and tornadoes and "earthquicks." I suggested that sometimes we don't see the whole picture, that there may be a purpose to things we can't understand. I compared our perspective to that of an ant. Think about the size of our driveway, I said, and of the world and of the universe to us as compared to an ant. Your mom said, "It would take an ant about five whole minutes to walk up the driveway, but I would do it in fifty seconds."

She began to muse on dying. She said she'd like to try it to see what it's like, as long as she could come back. I told her maybe that's what death is, a momentary leaving and then coming back to life. She asked me if she'd be able to see Chad, her cousin who had died in a car accident a few months before. I told her she might, and she might even meet my dad and my grandparents. I told her that she asked good questions. When I recounted this conversation to Grandpa, he said, "She makes connections."

About a month after this talk, Grandma Dee Ewing died of a heart attack at the age of seventy. Your mom didn't want to see her in the casket, and she stayed with Dee's friend Audra that evening. That night she posed many more good questions. She wanted to know the names and particulars of all the people who came to the calling hours, all about caskets, Grandma's hair and makeup, and burial. She dealt with a lot of death for such a little girl: her cousin Chad, Grandma Ewing, her cousin Karen (also killed in a car crash), and a year later my mom, her Grandma Miller.

There was no umbrella to shield her. I could only try to meet the challenge of her many excellent questions.

V Is for Vase

I HAVE LITTLE TO SAY ABOUT VASES. WHEN MY FRIEND Marianne, an avid gardener, sees the page in your finished book, she thinks V is for violets because purple flowers pour out from the vase. A timelier V word would be *vaccines*, which have been successfully developed for the coronavirus as I write and are beginning to be rolled out. The first recipient, other than the brave people in the clinical trials, is Margaret Keenan, a ninety-year-old British woman who received the Pfizer vaccine on December 8, 2020.

Our vaccines determine when we will see you in person. After staying indoors and avoiding restaurants, concerts, and family get-togethers, we aren't about to blow it by catching the virus on a plane to New York City. Acquiring the shot is the sticking point.

We registered with University Hospitals here in Cleveland in January 2021, to receive a vaccine when they become available. We heard nothing for weeks. Meantime, friends our age were beginning to be vaccinated in February. I scout the websites of drugstores and hospitals for available appointments. After a first dose of Pfizer vaccine, you receive a second dose three weeks later. Two weeks after that, you're fully immune. That means waiting five weeks after our first appointment, theoretically, to fly to New York. In the meantime, we determine with your mom that we aim to visit when you babies are about two weeks old. So many variables! Your due date is March 27. If you are born on your due date (like your cooperative Uncle Doug), our visit would commence around April 10.

But chances are good that you'll be early. If you're born in mid-March instead, the two-week time frame would make our arrival about March 30.

So the longer it takes to schedule a vaccine appointment, the less likely it is that we will see you before you are a month or so old. Like many other people, I spent hours online during those weeks, trying to scare up appointment times.

One day in February my friend Robin posts on Facebook that Rite Aid has appointments available, and I snag two for February 20. What a relief to have successfully traversed the Internet space to those appointments! Then comes a gigantic winter storm across much of the country, notably in Texas, and Rite Aid, unable to acquire vaccines, abruptly changes our appointments to March 13, which seems like a long wasteland of waiting. We won't meet you until the end of April!

Heartsick, I returned to the computer screen. I haunt Walgreen's website because friends have received Walgreen's vaccines. I even lurk at our nearest Walgreens pharmacy in person, hoping to snag a leftover dose at the end of the day, which is either a realistic possibility or an urban legend. Those Walgreens employees show me a saintly degree of patience.

Eventually I acquire a Walgreen's appointment on February 26, and after a lot more frustrated searching, one for your grandfather on March 3. We'll be good to travel in early April, shaving a little time off that cautious two-week wait after a second shot.

So now it's up to you guys. The longer you stay in utero, the better for you and the better for us. Your mom may disagree.

That night your grandfather and I watch a 1996 film called *Voci nel Tempo*, or *Voices through Time*. It has no plot and no dialogue, which is not unusual for some of the art movies that your grandfather chooses to watch. This one portrays a small Italian town and its people at all stages of life. The first shots are of a little baby, the iteration in which you two will soon appear. There follows footage of young children playing and dancing. Eventually we see teenagers, then a wedding, and then old people attending the wedding. There's a great deal of dancing and singing. The people's faces are lovingly shot, including hard-won wrinkles etched on the elders' faces.

With no dialogue (no need for subtitles!) and no plot, the filmmaker, Franco Piavoli, is after something apart from narrative. He's capturing the beauty, joy, and sadness of the life cycle in this village. That's the message, as long as you acknowledge that "enjoying" also incorporates the sting of loss and regret.

As you grow older, you become aware of how quickly time passes. You're in utero now, and time may seem to be passing slowly to your parents, so excited to meet you. But in twenty years, these nine months will seem more like one month, and in fifty years, they'll have contracted into a few moments. Your mom's entire childhood has telescoped in my mind into a short film projected at breakneck speed.

Near the end of *Voci nel Tempo*, an old guy rows a boat down a foggy river into shadows, and your grandfather says to me, "Charon. How do you pronounce that?" He means the mythological boatman who rowed souls across the River Styx into the underworld after death. (The correct pronunciation is just like the name "Karen.") I expect the film to end with that evocative shot, but instead a startling scene of little children shouting Italian words and laughing, running through a gate into the town square, ensues. Bright red coats and sunshine contrast with the grayness of the gloomy boatman. The kids are pulling sleds and running up a hill, and then more of the children end up at an iced-over pond and slide back and forth around each other. As that's happening, very soft violins are plucked in the background.

The volume increases, and you recognize the music as Pachelbel's Canon. An adult and child holding hands enter the frame and cross the icy pond amid the children who gradually disappear off frame. You're watching the duo walk off toward the horizon, the icy grays turning the film to black and white again as Pachelbel's music grows louder. The old human and the young human are silhouetted against the sky, with mountains on the distant horizon. The credits roll as the music, now at full volume, continues.

Pachelbel's Canon is a familiar piece of classical music. In dozens of movies and at thousands of weddings, it's been borrowed and lifted and covered, overused for decades. But I didn't know about its overuse the first time I heard it. Though I wouldn't call your grandfather jaded, he brought me up short the first time I ever heard it, almost fifty years ago.

We were flying to Seattle on our honeymoon on June 11, 1978, the day after our wedding. At twenty-six, I had flown before, but not often and never so far from home. Everything had a veneer of shiny newness: the long flight, being married, this guy John beside me, now my husband. I was even wearing a new outfit. Your great-grandmother Dee had bought me a traveling suit. She loved to buy me clothes. "Young girls should wear bright colors," she would say. The outfit consisted of a pink blazer and wrap-around skirt and a patterned t-shirt to go with it. Even so long ago wearing a new outfit for traveling was very retro—I lived in blue jeans. But it was a nice ensemble, purchased specially for the trip, and so I wore it. There's a snapshot of me sitting at the gate before the flight, pretty in pink.

Flying back then was luxurious. The flight attendants (called stewardesses, and all women) brought you snacks and drinks and also full meals on a cross-country flight. Grandpa had shared his excitement with me about the in-flight meal. He loved the neat little containers and the surprise about what the meal would be. Every seat offered headphones with channels for different sorts of music. I chose the classical channel, put on the headphones, and looked out the window to my right. Amid a brilliant blue sky and billowy floating clouds, ethereal music entered me through the headphones. The music ran on a loop, so I put the headphones on several times on that long flight in order to hear it again. By the second or third time, the music was making me tear up. It represented everything about the moment to me. The excitement and freshness of my new life were in that view out the window and that otherworldly music entering my ears.

I nudged Grandpa to give him a listen. He said, "Pachelbel. You've never heard that before? It's everywhere."

His comment was only mildly deflating. Too bad I couldn't share my bliss with him, but I savored the experience for myself alone. Recalling this experience at the end of *Voci nel Tempo*, I realize that airborne moment held everything that came after. Marriage. Our lives. Your mom. And now you yourselves, also traceable to that moment. Your mom tells me that babies in utero practice breathing to strengthen their lungs, which I never knew. Swimming in utero as I write, soon to take in real air, to go to school, to play with dogs, to grow big (everything I hope for) can be tracked to that moment thousands of feet in the air with Pachelbel's Canon—overused and sublime— as graceful soundtrack.

W Is for Whale

YOUR GRANDFATHER AND I READ *MOBY-DICK* AT THE SAME time in the 1970s. We also read *War and Peace* together when we were dating. I used to accuse him of bait and switch, because soon after we married, or maybe after we became engaged, he pretty much stopped reading. In actual fact, he read a lot—*Film Comment, Variety, Sight and Sound*, and other film publications—but not so much the novels and other literature I wanted him to read. Beginning a couple of years ago, he's picked up reading again. He made a resolution, I guess. He reads mostly classics so as not to waste his time. Right now we're both reading *To the Lighthouse* by Virginia Woolf.

Your cousin Frances, a sophomore at Smith College, is reading *Moby-Dick* as I write this. I read it first at Kent State in 1974 when I took a course in Melville with Howard Vincent (aka Moby Vincent), an eminent Melville scholar and star of the English faculty. He wrote critical studies of Melville, such as *The Tailoring of White Jacket* and *The Trying-Out of Moby-Dick*. His theme, as the titles indicate, was the creative process. In fact, that was the name of one of his course offerings, in which we read *The Act of Creation* by Arthur Koestler.

He used to refer to the "cetological center" of *Moby-Dick*—that is, the vast number of words in the middle of the book devoted to the habits and physiology of whales. That part of the book stalls a lot of people. I've cautioned my book group members, who occasionally suggest reading it, "There's an awful lot about whaling in there, you know." Just like there's a lot about farming in *War and Peace* and a lot about architecture in *The Hunchback of Notre Dame*. If you crave adventure stories, be forewarned. These great books contain a lot of other stuff.

Every professor has a hobby horse. Dr. Vincent's was the work of writing itself. He always connected our assigned readings to that theme, asserting that whatever writers were writing about, they were also writing about writing. When Melville's Bartleby the Scrivener says, "I would prefer not to," he's representing Melville himself, who had wearied of writing the popular whaling sagas he'd outgrown. Novels can be about a spooky house with seven gables in Salem, Massachusetts (which Grandpa also recently read), or about a magnificent white whale, but the theme of writing and creating throbs underneath—always. The artist Lily Briscoe serves that purpose in *To the Lighthouse*. I'm sharing this idea because I've found it a useful way to look at the fiction I read.

Moby-Dick, your grandpa tells me, was the first movie he couldn't see. (He can't remember the first movie he did see.) As a child, he was obsessed with whales like some kids are obsessed with dinosaurs. Even now, he dearly loves Walt Disney's *Pinocchio*, in large part because Monstro the whale scared and fascinated him. In 1956, when Grandpa was five years old, his older brothers went off to see the *Moby-Dick* movie starring Gregory Peck and directed by John Huston. (Grandpa's future idol, Orson Welles, was in it too.) Grandpa begged to go along but was not allowed because he was too young. He can't remember if he cried and fussed, but because the subject has periodically come up in our forty-three years of marriage, I know that this injustice still rankles.

Your book's whale is another fictional whale, not much like a real wrinkled whale, encrusted with barnacles. The smooth gray, dotted fabric comes from the project making placemats for your mom and dad a few years ago. The ocean water is, of course, blue. The whale's big eye gazes at us impishly, and the huge W, made from a turquoise print, arises from the whale's head.

Charlemagne's scribes created that W in around 900 AD. They put two Us next to each other, which were actually shaped like Vs, and called it "double-u." The French call it a "double-v." No matter what you call it, it has the familiar W sound.

The sound begins *washing*. This has been a watchword of the pandemic. Handwashing, handwashing, handwashing. At least twenty seconds at a time! The time it takes to sing "Happy Birthday" twice. Presumably, if everyone washed more carefully, transmission of all sorts of bugs would diminish, including E-coli and ordinary cold viruses.

At the beginning of the pandemic, doctors didn't know precisely how the virus spread and cautioned us to beware of surfaces. Through much of this time, friends have had groceries delivered to the house and leave the bags outside for a while, hoping the virus dissipates. They wash the packages when they come into the kitchen. A friend of mine washes all her produce in soapy water. They leave the mail sitting for hours on the coffee table. Throughout the day, we wash our hands. On a pandemic blog created by friends in my writing group, I wrote about this washing obsession.

> But then, at any given time, I become conscious merely of my hands: when did I wash them last? What if my hands are infecting the plastic bag holding the apples? Do I wash my hands before I open the bag and touch the apple, or do I wash them after I open the bag and touch the apple, but before I actually eat the apple?

Hand washing continues, though the advice has changed somewhat. From the early days in March 2020, Dr. Fauci assured us that surfaces pose little risk, but he can't say no risk. Within a few months, it became clear that the virus travels via aerosol, and the air poses a greater danger by far. Soon we are all about the masks, and at the same time we try to continue the washing. Maybe that good habit will stick around for a while.

I've been thinking of another W: *West Side Story*, the 1957 musical by Leonard Bernstein and Stephen Sondheim. Currently, a new film version directed by Steven Spielberg is appearing. For a time in 1994, when your mom was eight, it was all the rage in our house. We had watched a PBS production on TV and then checked out the compact disc at the library. When we brought it home, I couldn't slide it into the player soon enough. Your mom set the stereo to "scramble," and then switched every song as it came on because she was so excited to hear all of them. To "Officer Krupke"—a funny, bouncy song—your mom and Doug cavorted and hopped all around the living room. They leapt from the couch to chairs, trying to sing along with the fast-paced lyrics.

We had also checked out a book with all the words (no Google searching back then!). The kids decided they wanted to sing the "Quintet," the song that precedes the big rumble between the show's gang members. Our singing became pretty chaotic, not to say acrimonious. By the exciting end, the two gangs, Tony, Maria, and Anita are all singing at once. I pointed out that the three of us were trying to sing five parts (by definition) and should switch to something simpler. "We quit in disorder," I wrote in my journal.

Then your mom wanted to pick out some of the melodies on the piano. She chose "Cool," an appealing choice but beyond my skills to help her figure out. I suggested switching to "One Hand" with its straightforward melody. Your mom asked me to write it out for her on a staff because she could read the notes. At bedtime we once again sang some of the songs as I lay with your mom in bed.

West Side Story mania raged on for a few weeks.

More recently, your mom and dad have been infatuated, along with the rest of the world, with another musical, Lin Manuel Miranda's *Hamilton*. For our fortieth wedding anniversary in 2018, they surprised us with tickets to the road show in Cleveland, and, even better, they flew here to attend with us. Your dad likes to brag that he saw it first, in previews, with some of his students. Your mom chaperoned some of her students to see it a couple years later. At that performance, notably, the writer Toni Morrison sat a few seats in front of them and posed for pictures with your mom's charges, who coincidentally were reading her early novel *The Bluest Eye* at the time.

I picture some day in the future when your mom and dad will watch you two wheel and whirl around your living room to Alexander Hamilton belting out "My Shot."

X Is for Xylophone

YOUR BOOK'S TOY XYLOPHONE HAS TWO HAMMERS, BUT only four notes. I used to have one like it as a child with only one hammer but eight notes because eight notes form a whole octave and make a few melodies possible. The tunes had to be in the key of C because there were no sharps and flats. I could handle "Jingle Bells," which I remember chanting to myself, "3-3-3. 3-3-3. 3-5-1-2-3."

I hope you learn to play real instruments someday. I played the trombone in junior high and high school. I used to say that I chose it to meet boys because it was perceived as a masculine instrument, but really, I was always fascinated by the slide and wanted to learn where to start and stop it to find the notes. Your dad was quite a good trumpet player. One time he let slip a comment that inadvertently reveals how smart and capable he is: he remarked that he could have made music his major. Your Aunt Ashley attended college on a trumpet scholarship. Your mom took guitar lessons and had a natural aptitude for music too. She used to play our piano for fun and learned how to play Vanessa Carlton's "A Thousand Miles," a pop song she liked. She felt impatient with me when I found this impressive, but I tried and struggled with playing piano and never progressed beyond rudimentary, halting exercises. Grandpa never learned to play anything, but I think he would have been good at it also. Your great-uncle David played the accordion.

I like that most of the images in your book are not toys but real things, whatever that means. They're crude representations of real things, anyway; except for the bear, which is clearly a teddy bear, and the yoyo, a quintessential toy. Now that I look over it, though, I see the kite as well.

The word *xylophone* is a Greek compound: *xylum*, meaning "wood," plus *phonos*, meaning "sound." The xylophone bars are, etymologically speaking, always made of wood. Sound words are common, such as *telephone* and *phonograph* and *homophone*. A tree's xylem is the woody tissue that transports minerals and water from the roots.

(Your uncle Doug humorously suggested X stand for all of your great-aunts' ex-husbands. I could have stitched a little row of male figures, totaling around five.)

The Greek X was called *chi* (X). Greek organizations, or fraternities and sororities, are one of the only ways people today see or learn Greek letters. Why did they use Greek letters for their names? In a word, pretentiousness.

Until about the middle of the twentieth century, young men had to study Latin and Greek in order to be considered educated. Often they could take Latin in high school, but Greek was usually reserved for the university. It was considered more difficult (its own alphabet and all) and more prestigious even than Latin. When an honorary club for elite students formed in 1776 at William and Mary College, it used Greek letters *Phi Beta Kappa*, which stood for its motto, Philosophy the Guide of Life. Soon other organizations followed suit, devising a Greek motto from the first letters of each word to name the fraternity. Often the underlying Greek motto was kept a secret except to members.

After a while, the mottos faded away, and fraternities and the sororities that followed used random Greek letters for their names. *Frater* in Latin means "brother" and *soror* means "sister." In fact, *chi*, the letter that looks like our X, appears in the name of your mom's sorority, *Alpha Chi Omega*. Your dad's college fraternity too: *Sigma Chi*.

This letter explains the derivation of one of my favorite poetic and rhetorical devices—chiasmus. It's so much my favorite that students weary of my explaining it and providing examples. Sometimes when I ask a class to look closely at a line of Latin poetry, they automatically cross their arms in front of them to make an X.

Chiasmus is a kind of switcheroo. The speaker or writer says something and then in the next phrase reverses the order of the words. When I was in college, a professor explained that John F. Kennedy's classically educated speech writers knew what they were doing when they wrote, "Ask not what your country can do for you. Ask what you can do for your country." Classic chiasmus. To show us where the *chi* comes in, he wrote the lines on the blackboard, with the second line under the first. Then he connected the two *yous* and the two *countrys*, forming a great big X on the board. The line is famous, he explained, not merely because of its sentiment, but because of its memorable crafting. It's not just that you make an alphabet book, but that you (try to) make it well.

My refrigerator currently sports a magnet, a gift from my friend Judi, that says, "It's not that diamonds are a girl's best friend. It's that your best friends are diamonds." A familiar admonition suggests that if you can't be with the one you love, then you love the one you're with. The witches in Shakespeare's Macbeth said, "Fair is foul, and foul is fair." I am attuned to seeing chiasmus in print and in speech, as my students, Grandpa, and Uncle Doug will attest. They have no idea how often I have noted a chiasmus and generously let it pass, having learned that not everyone will find it as interesting as I do.

Chi has another common use. For centuries it has stood for Christ because in Greek that "ch" is written with a *chi*, or X. When conservative Christians occasionally rail that Xmas is "taking the Christ out of Christmas," they're mistaken. The X is merely a traditional abbreviation for Christ.

Christmas 2020 is approaching while I am working on this page. Sadly, though it is the Christmas for your mom and dad to travel to Cleveland, COVID put the kibosh on their visit. Very few people are flying. Your mom can hardly be expected to ride ten hours in a car when she is pregnant with you little rascals. Precautions are in order because the coronavirus is particularly dangerous for pregnant women. I've been suppressing my own concerns about that ever since I learned about you in September. The pandemic has its ups and downs. Maybe they can come to Cleveland? But then, no, it's too dangerous.

Because they definitely aren't coming to Cleveland, I wrap some presents to send to your mom and dad in New York. A bundle covered in brown paper labeled "Baby 1 and Baby 2" contains clothes I've kept in the attic for over thirty years, hoping for a time I could share them with grandchildren. About twenty years ago, I sorted through the stash and gave away a lot, so the collection I have is not too overwhelming for me or for your mom, who likes nice things and might feel ambivalent about old clothes. Because they're so small, she has no reason to feel sentimental about them; she doesn't remember wearing them or seeing her brother Doug wearing them. I'm the one with my heart in my throat.

The foundation of the package is a soft pink blanket with little bears embroidered on the corners. All the pink items, of course, were purchased for your mom. This pretty blanket seems almost brand new. There's also a smaller pink receiving blanket. There's a white terrycloth onesie that belonged to Uncle Doug, a blue patterned gown, and another gown with a pink collar and delicate flowers that I loved very much.

The last and most sentimental item is a onesie that looks like a baseball uniform. From the waist up it's white with blue stripes and from the waist down it's blue.

When Uncle Doug was born, I had to stay in the hospital for a few days.

Back then, they had just begun the practice of sending moms and babies home after one night. I had bled quite a bit, though, and Doug had the hiccups, and so they decided to keep us a little longer. Your great-grandparents Stan and Dee visited us in Canton's Aultman Hospital, and Stan came bearing that baseball onesie. He was a quiet guy, not usually prone to sharing his emotions. But his face shone with tears as he handed that little present to me, along with a plush toy baseball. Doug was his first grandson, and Stan was the biggest Cleveland Indians fan ever.

Though he lived in Canton, an hour away, Stan had season tickets to all the home games in Cleveland. For a long time, in fact, he bought eight seats. As owner of a car dealership, he shared the tickets with customers and employees. Aunt Penni, Uncle David, daughter Amy, and Aunt Barbara and her family came up to games. We, too, were beneficiaries, sitting in prime seats a few rows behind the Indians dugout in their new stadium, then called Jacobs Field. As a season ticket holder, Stan also had first crack at playoff and World Series and All-Star games, which he shared with us.

In 1991 Stan took our family to Tucson to see the Indians in spring training. Eight-year-old Doug learned to approach those giant athletes, a magazine or paper and pen in hand, and ask for autographs. Somewhere around here we have an old spring-training magazine filled with indecipherable signatures from obscure players who never made it to the big leagues.

We attended Game 4 of the 1995 World Series between the Indians and the Atlanta Braves (your dad's team of choice). I recall your nine-year-old mom's heartfelt sympathy for the young pitcher, Julian Tavares, who was in tears when we lost. Like all Cleveland fans, we were crushed when the normally reliable Jose Mesa blew a ninth-inning lead in the seventh game of the 1997 World Series. We attended the fourth game of that one, too, for which Grandpa made a big sign that said, "Teal, Schmiel," ridiculing the Marlin's bright aqua uniforms. Our sign no doubt helped us win the game, despite the cold. That October day saw snow in Cleveland, and we shivered in our field box seats. The next day's *Plain Dealer* sports page exulted, "Win Chill Factor."

After that initial baseball-related gift, which I realize now that Grandma Dee probably purchased, Stan shared his love of baseball with all his grandchildren, forming a particularly devoted fan in Doug, who, like Stan, follows all sports avidly. Both your mom and Doug played softball with a community league, and your mom played softball in high school. Your dad, as you no doubt know, was a skilled pitcher who was scouted for the minor leagues, until he smashed his shoulder sliding into second, ending his serious baseball chances.

Ball-playing brought your parents together, in fact, as the *New York Times* noted on July 10, 2016, in one of their "Vows" stories about weddings. Your parents are pictured outside an ice cream shop devouring cones.

(There's that I for ice cream again.) Vinnie from the *New York Times*, as he identified himself when he called to interview them, reported that they were married on July 9 and met, according to the headline, "fraternizing with the opposition."

The story explains that your parents were coaches of opposing high-school teams. Your dad coached first base and flirted with your mom. His fellow coach ran up the score, ending 11-0, and your dad was afraid your mom would think he was a jerk. Your dad sent your mom an email at her school inviting her for coffee. She was seeing another guy at the time, but that relationship didn't last long, and she remembered your dad. When she broke up with the other guy, she contacted your dad and said she was ready for that coffee. Which turned out to be a drink at a Manhattan bar. And the rest is history.

My own mom and dad attended Indians games when they were dating. My mom used to say they experienced the thrill of seeing Satchel Paige pitch, although by the time he joined the Indians they were married, with kids, in Canton. They must have seen him play in an exhibition game before that. I'd sit in the living room as a kid watching Indians games on our floor model Motorola TV with my dad. These were the days of Woody Held, Larry Brown, Tito Francona, Jimmy Piersall, and Sam McDowell. My dad spent the last twenty years of his life in a wheelchair, due to complications after a spinal abscess, and would sit with one limp leg dangling over the armrest and a bottle of Iron City beer tucked into the wheelchair beside him. Every now and then, he'd explain the infield fly rule to me, a lesson not many girls my age learned from their dads.

As I write, it's being announced that after next year, the Indians will no longer be called the Indians. Chief Wahoo has pretty much been discontinued, though he still adorns many hats and shirts in our neck of the woods. The disappearance is part of a welcome trend, which has picked up steam in this year of Black Lives Matter, to examine the racism embedded in so many of our traditions and so many of our hearts.

One of the many ways your lives will differ from ours will be growing up in a world with a Cleveland baseball team, but no Cleveland Indians.

Y Is for Yoyo

As I've explained, these pages are wonkily assembled in a perfectly logical arrangement, discernible only if you are perfectly logical. The Z coming up next was one of the first pages I made up, with A on its facing side. This Y page appears side by side with the B. And so on.

As the end of the book approaches, I spend part of the day practicing making buttonholes. The pattern prescribes that a shoelace woven through buttonholes will secure the pages. Lacking confidence in my buttonholing skills, I ask my friend Judi for the names of some seamstresses. Judi's the organized sort of person who might hire someone to do alterations. Writing this, I realize that *seamstress* seems like an antiquated term. Online, *seamists* sometimes appears instead, but that word is not recognized by dictionaries yet, nor by my word processing program. *Sewer* is an accepted and long-standing non-gendered alternative, but at first glance it appears plumbing-related. At this point in time, there is no adequate politically correct alternative.

In a last-ditch effort to be self-reliant, I try grommets on some fabric remnants, but because of all the hammering and fraying, I give up on them. One must go with a technique that works. That is, a technique that isn't too unsightly and amateurish and is also sturdy. I resolve to call one of Judi's experts, a Croatian lady who owns a small business in Eastlake, which would involve a bit of a drive.

But after a few days of practice, I feel more confident. I create four decent buttonholes on a mock page, relying on the sewing machine's handbook. Then I watch a couple of YouTube videos that offer helpful hints. For example, when you rip out the middle of the buttonhole, you attach a pin crosswise at one end to make sure you don't rip right through one end of the stitching. My major remaining concern is making each buttonhole the same size. Some machine's buttonhole foots (feet?) have a gizmo that automatically measures the buttonhole to the size of your button. My machine lacks that gizmo. I think the trick, as with many things I'm learning about, is to prepare carefully. One can draw a buttonhole as a line with ends marked in the shape of an I. Methinks I need to practice the measuring a little more.

One of the women on YouTube says that buttonholes strike fear into even experienced seamstresses, sewists, and seamists because they're usually the final step, and you can ruin the entire garment right at the end by screwing up the buttonholes. Yikes. She said it out loud. That's exactly what I'm afraid of.

I won't have time to practice today. It's Thanksgiving, and I'm making a big dinner for Grandpa, Doug, and me. The pandemic has prohibited family gatherings! Yesterday I made stuffing, a pumpkin pie, and a broccoli cheese casserole that's a staple for us on Thanksgiving and Christmas. I just now put a twenty-four-pound turkey in the oven. I know, that's ginormous, especially for three people, especially when one of them is a vegetarian. Doug received the bird free at work, and Grandpa and I infer that he really wants to provide for our turkey needs. Also, Doug doesn't feel appreciated at work and probably feels that he deserves a free turkey. As a vegetarian, I have pretty much forsworn cooking whole turkeys, which I have routinely done for our Christmas Eve dinners with my side of the family. I switched to turkey breast last year and was going to stick with that. But here I am this morning, yanking the half-frozen neck and giblets out of the turkey's inside and almost retching at the sight of the stump of the neck on the turkey where the head was detached. I am not judgmental of people who eat meat. I ate meat into my forties and have no grounds to judge others. But I'll say this—I lay in bed for a while last night feeling sad and guilty about the large dead animal in our refrigerator. And I feel actual nausea this morning while preparing it.

I'm thinking once again of Grandma Ewing, my mother-in-law Dee, as I frequently do around the holidays. I have been recalling how many Thanksgivings and Christmases she got up early to prepare stuffing and wrangle a turkey into the oven because the family ate their holiday meals around noon. She also peeled potatoes and made pies and put together vegetable casseroles. Guests like me brought some dishes, but most of the holiday preparations rested entirely on her shoulders, year after year. I always appreciated what she did but never more than now.

Yesterday a chef who'd written a book about his family and his work in restaurants was interviewed on *Fresh Air*, a National Public Radio program. He's an admitted workaholic and is working on his recovery, which the pandemic is ironically helping him with. The host, Terry Gross, asked him if he cooks for his family. He laughed and said that chefs rarely cook at home because they're so sick of cooking. Lots of takeout, she said, and he laughed and agreed. Now he has a baby, who along with the pandemic is helping him change. He cooks at home. He said, "I never experienced preparing food as an act of love for your family before." I have been thinking about that comment ever since.

I hope not to sound too martyrlike when I say that nearly every day I experience preparing food as an act of love for my family. Sure, sometimes dinner preparations are slapdash, occasionally seasoned with a dash of resentment. Even so, plenty of times I'm thinking of the future diners as I cook and hoping they like what I make. I prepare things I don't like or won't eat for them. It's weird to me that the chef never experienced this feeling before now.

Which brings me back to Dee Ewing, your great-grandmother. She too was sometimes resentful and often stressed and exhausted during the holidays. Some of us surmised that she suffered her fatal heart attack on December 6 because she just couldn't face another Christmas season. I think Valium sometimes came to her aid over the years as she labored over her massive shopping, wrapping, and cooking extravaganzas. This morning I'm thankful that she expressed her love for all of us and would for you if she were here to do it. She made holidays happen, standing in her robe and slippers early in the morning, wrestling a huge turkey into a roasting pan, her mind running in a thousand directions about all the other items on her to-do list.

You can see I don't have much to say about yoyos, but I can tell you about Y. Its ancestor Egyptian hieroglyph represented a supporting pole. The Semites named it *waw*, their word for *hook*. It retained the same shape but metamorphosed into four other letters, as we have seen: F, U, V, and W.

Y always reminds me of my friend Chris's email address, which contains *yggidrasil*—in Norse mythology a great and sacred tree. But the Y can also stand for *yogurt*. When Christmas rolls around, I will be receiving an Instant Pot from your mom. By January 2021, I will, after eight hours of steeping, have made my own yogurt.

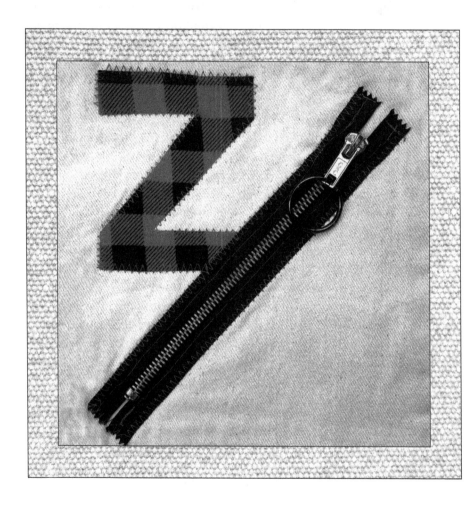

Z Is for Zipper

Z DERIVES FROM *ZETA* (Z), THE SIXTH LETTER OF THE Greek alphabet. Another name for our zee is *zed*, evidence of its connection to its Greek ancestor. The American pronunciation, zee, dates from the 1670s or so. Z, the last letter entered into the Latin alphabet, wasn't needed for native Latin words but appeared only in Greek loan words, such as *zephyr*, the west wind, and *azalea*, a genus of flowers. The line from Scripture goes, "I am the *Alpha* and *Omega*." *Omega* was the Greeks' final letter. In modern terms, God would say, "I am the A and the Z." but that lacks a certain poetic ring.

For this page, I use a zipper foot for my first time ever in order to attach the zipper to the page. One of my learning leaps! The sewing machine part holding the fabric in place under the needle is called the presser foot. The zipper foot attachment also secures the fabric but on only one side of the needle, not both, so that you can stitch close to the metal teeth of the zipper. First, I follow my own advice and look up directions for attaching the zipper foot in the handbook. The handbook contains no such directions. I also must actually locate the zipper foot, tucked into a little drawer with other sewing machine attachments I never use. I fiddle around with the presser foot myself and discover a little lever at the back. When I move it, the presser foot startles me by falling off.

The zipper foot attaches in its place pretty easily. I fasten the zipper with both straight stitches and then zigzag stitches—a double Z word! The pattern advises me to stitch securely at each end to enable babies to pull the zipper up and down, which I hope you both do a lot. I have already bought an extra big zipper pull—a gold key chain from our local hardware store—so that baby hands can grasp it easily.

The letter Z itself causes me some difficulty because the thread suddenly starts breaking. Sometimes I can figure out a cause for such headaches but often just have to plow through. After much stopping and rethreading, eventually the stitching proceeds smoothly. I practice not catastrophizing.

I work on this page early in the process, as I've said, at the same time as A, beginning around Halloween 2020. It's hard to enter into the spirit of any holiday during this pandemic, and I am not sure we'll be handing out candy. I buy candy just in case, but I don't decorate. In the afternoon of Halloween, your grandpa carves a pumpkin, as he does every year. He spreads newspapers out on the kitchen floor and uses his special little orange serrated knife. Roxie is plenty interested because seedy wet pumpkin insides definitely smell like food, even though she finds them unappealing sniffed up close. Grandpa removes the screen from the front door, so that when we open the inside door the little goblins are right there in front of us. Then we can insert the storm window—needed for the cold weather—as the evening ends. Our box of decorations from the attic has sat on the living room floor for several weeks. It looks like it will return to the attic undisturbed.

Your mother finally returns my phone calls on Halloween. (And if *finally* sounds snarky, good.) I want to offer to pay for a doula for her childbirth experience, or a postpartum doula, or a night nurse, or some combination. She is appreciative and, with her customary thoroughness, is already exploring options. The rest of the time we talk about her school preparations for returning to in-person learning on November 4. Because of COVID and the dire situation in NYC during the spring, many school buildings are closed, and students are connecting with classes and teachers remotely. Your mom's school is soon opening for four days a week, and students will take turns attending only one day a week. The restrictions are draconian. Students, limited to about fifteen, will remain in one classroom all day, wearing masks. At lunchtime they'll move to the back of the classroom and sanitize their hands. During that time, the teacher will spray and wipe down all the desks. The kids will return to their desks with their lunches, remove their masks, and eat. When finished, they'll throw out the trash in the back of the room and clean their hands again. The teacher will sanitize their desks again. Then students will return to their desks with their masks.

Although the scientists are now telling us that surfaces are not so dangerous, everyone feels reassured by a lot of sanitizing.

Also in the afternoon, Grandpa and I take a Halloween Day walk in Lakeview Cemetery, a beautiful parklike place near us, about 285 acres, that is 150 years old this year. We take Roxie, wearing her little brown sweater because it's chilly, though sunny and crisp. Bright yellow maples and a gorgeous red oak gleam in the sunshine. We stroll up and down some hills, hoping to avoid losing our way, which is easy to do. History is all around. We see one monument for a Thorndike family that commemorates sons lost at Gettysburg in 1863 and at Andersonville prison in 1864.

Three young women stop us to ask if we know where the Angel of Death is. I know the statue they're talking about but don't know the winding roads of the cemetery well enough to give directions. Their phones tell them they're in the right section. They also ask the location of the grave of Eliot Ness, *The Untouchables* crime fighter. We can't help them. They tell us our dog is cute. We return to the car, and on our way out we find the Angel, near Daffodil Hill, which your grandfather mistakenly calls Dandelion Hill. I say he is thinking of our yard.

We spot the girls driving by in their car and try to tell them how to find the Angel. They seem confused, so I suggest we lead them back to where the Angel is. We are uncertain we can find it ourselves, but we do. We point it out to them through the window, wave, and drive away. COVID hovers over our encounter. We keep our distance from the girls and vice versa. We even have to shout a little to be heard. Even so, we enjoy a safe, outdoor, cordial exchange with strangers—an unusual experience these days.

I ask Grandpa if he chose to walk at Lakeview because it's Halloween, but he says no, it's just because he knows that the trees are pretty. Which they are. I hope it's not too morbid to suggest that the two of us might be lying there at Lakeview now as you read this. We've talked about buying plots there. Or rather I've talked about it. Grandpa likes to change the subject when I bring it up.

For right now, though, I seize the wolf by the ears and commence the buttonholes. I try calling Judi's contact, but her hours are restricted, and I never get around to calling back. The half-hour drive to Eastlake is daunting, as is conferring with a stranger during a pandemic. And so is driving back to Eastlake when the book is finished.

I practice stitching a row of four buttonholes on scraps of the canvas fabric that makes up the book. I rip them open and weave a shoelace through them. That all works. Next is deciding what color thread to use around the buttonholes. I could make them all the same. The dark green I use for practice would look neutral and tasteful and has the advantage of neither breaking nor puckering; sometimes when you change thread you create problems for yourself. I decide to use it first on the pages where it appears around the edges, which includes the frog page, which is, as you know, green. That is my first page of buttonholes.

I realize after completing another page of buttonholes (red thread for the B page) that I have been figuring the numbers all wrong, quailing at the idea of forty-eight buttonholes. But of course it isn't forty-eight buttonholes.

There are seven joined pages all told, four buttonholes apiece, making twenty-eight buttonholes. Much less intimidating. Also they go pretty smoothly once you get the hang of it.

I use orange buttonholes for the orange-trimmed penguin page. The first one is a disaster—okay on the front but jumbled with knots and snarls on the back. I trim some of the messy thread, wondering if the whole thing will eventually unravel. I rip it out and start again. These buttonhole stitches are thick and tight, and my little seam ripper has to work long and hard to pull them out. Eventually, I redo these buttonholes, and they look much better.

Appropriately enough, this Z page is the site of our last buttonhole, the bottom one that shows on the cover. The last step before laundering is weaving in the shoelace that ties it all together. The book is more or less completed before Christmas.

•

On March 5, 2021, I am writing this chapter when I receive a cryptic text from your mom. It says, "Hi! I have an update from the doc this morning, so I wanted to fill you in."

I call as soon as I see it. Your mom answers from a hospital bed, hooked up to monitors. The doctor has advised that because you both aren't growing very fast, especially Boy Baby, they would induce labor today. "At this point, they're better off outside than inside," your mom summarizes. Your dad's job is to text me and your Grandma Connie (and probably lots of other less important people) as the day goes on.

A pitocin drip to induce labor begins in the afternoon. The hours drag by with intermittent (not enough!) text updates from your dad. Gentle contractions begin before I go to bed. I plug in my phone on my bedside table, which I never do. I text your dad that I have my phone at hand, instructing that he should apprise me of any developments during the night.

I sleep fitfully, checking my phone every hour or two. When I wake up at 7:15, I grab my phone and see, to my dismay, no messages. The minutes tick by, and I go to a dark place, certain that something bad has happened to one or both of you, or three of you, because why else would your dad not tell us in the morning that everything is okay? Because your dad has never been a mom, and because he actually believes, as he told us, that "no news is good news." I say just wait until this new baby girl is grown and giving birth hundreds of miles away from where he is. Then, I think peevishly, we'll see if no news is good news.

At 7:52 pm Grandma Connie texts your dad, "Any news?" A while later, I post, "Waiting. Tim?" About a half hour later, he responds, "Everyone is now here. All is good. Will send a more detailed update soon." Your aunts and grandma respond with excitement.

Finally there comes a picture of the two of you, side by side, facing in opposite directions as though you've had just about enough of each other, thank you very much. After a few text-screams from aunts and Grandma, your dad, with dignity and restraint, introduces you by name.

That's it. Thirty hours or so of labor. Thirty-seven weeks of waiting. Everyone is now here, as your dad says. You are the good news.

·

Almost forty years ago, Grandpa made up a baby announcement for your Uncle Doug, playing off a movie poster, because, well, movies. It's designed to look like the poster for *E.T. the Extra Terrestrial* and announces the premiere of "DE," for Doug Ewing. Underneath it says, "In his Adventure on Earth." I keep thinking of that line. Here you are now, both of you, in your adventure on earth.

Your mom's birth announcement was patterned after the poster for *Rocky IV*, which came out around the time of her birth in February of 1986. Her fighting spirit is frequently in evidence, not least in her carrying twins in a pandemic, continuing to teach, enduring thirty hours of labor, canoeing for three hours, reorganizing an entire household for your arrival, undergoing a C-section, and, eventually, taking care of you two jamokes.

Meanwhile, Grandpa and I have finally received the treasured shots that will allow us soon to travel safely to New York to meet you. The press is cautiously reporting that the end of the pandemic is in sight, almost exactly one year in, though we all remain skeptical. The end is not going to be the satisfying definitive ending we hoped for. Anxiety, grief, and suffering remain around the world. Our safety depends on people's care for other people, their openness to vaccines, and continuing vigilance.

We're waiting for our immune response to kick in. The hours pass slowly. On some nice March days, I sit on the porch and imagine holding you and deeply inhaling your sweet baby scent. While I wait, I scan the trees, looking to see if the blue jays are returning to their old nest.

About the Author

KATHY EWING taught Latin and English at Cleveland State University for twenty-four years. Her writing has appeared in *Belt, The Bark, Mother's Day Magazine, The Plain Dealer, America, The Millions, Brevity*, and *National Catholic Reporter*. She has published two previous books: *Missing: Coming to Terms with a Borderline Mother* (Red Giant Books, 2016) and *Lead Me, Guide Me: The Life and Example of Father Dan Begin* (Shanti Arts, 2020). She blogs at www.kathyewing.com.

Shanti Arts

Nature • Art • Spirit

Please visit us online
to browse our entire book catalog,
including poetry collections and fiction,
books on travel, nature, healing, art,
photography, and more.

Also take a look at our highly regarded art
and literary journal, *Still Point Arts Quarterly*,
which may be downloaded for free.

www.shantiarts.com

CPSIA information can be obtained
at www.ICGtesting.com
Printed in the USA
LVHW051804150623
749886LV00012B/1631